THE RULER
OF THE KINGS ON THE EARTH

A Clear Look at Amillennialism
for the Lay Person

R. G. Currell

and

E. P. Hurlbut

Presbyterian and Reformed Publishing Co.
Phillipsburg, New Jersey 08865

Copyright © 1982
R. G. Currell and E. P. Hurlbut

ISBN 0-87552-211-4

Printed in the United States of America

Except where indicated, Scripture quotations are from the New American Standard Bible, © The Lockman Foundation, 1960, 1962, 1963, 1968, 1971, 1972. Other Scripture citations are from: King James Version, the John C. Winston Company, © 1948; Revised Standard Version of the Bible, © 1946, 1952, 1971; New American Bible (notes and text), © 1970, Confraternity of Christian Doctrine, Washington, D.C.

Excerpts from *Revelation* translated with introduction and commentary by J. Massyngberde Ford. Copyright © 1975 by Doubleday & Company, Inc. Reprinted by permission of the publisher.

Excerpts from *The Revelation of John,* vols. 1 and 2, translated and interpreted by William Barclay. Published in the U.S.A. by the Westminster Press, 1961. Used by permission.

To Chuck, Beth, and Jenny

CONTENTS

PART I: AN INTRODUCTION
TO AMILLENNIAL INTERPRETATION
Why a Book on Amillennialism for Lay Persons? 3
The Proposition of This Book 4
Principles of Interpretation 6
 Moderation between Overliteralization and "Higher Criticism"
 The Contextual Method
 The New Testament Interprets the Old Testament

PART II: THE HISTORICAL AUTHENTICITY
OF AMILLENNIALISM
Preliminary Remarks 13
 The Distinction between Classical and
 Dispensational Premillennialism
A Look at History 16
 The Old Testament: Up to 400 B.C.
 The Intertestamental Period: 400 B.C. to Christ
 The New Testament
 The Post-Apostolic Era, Early Church Fathers: Before A.D. 325
 The Apologists: After A.D. 325
 The Dark (Middle) Ages: 500 to 1400
 The Reformation: 1400 to 1550
 The Seventeenth and Eighteenth Centuries: Postmillennialism
 The Nineteenth and Twentieth Centuries: Dispensationalism

PART III: TWENTY QUESTIONS ANSWERED
Preliminary Remarks 45
 1. **What Exactly Is the Kingdom of God?** 46
    Spiritual, Eternal Dominion; the Sovereignty of God
 2. **What Then Is the Difference between the
    Old Testament Kingdom and the New?** 49
    The Father's Kingdom: Jewish Israel; the Son's
    Kingdom: Gentile Church

v

3. **What Exactly Is Meant by the Word "Millennium"?** . 50
   Linguistic Roots; Redefinition of Nature and Chronology
4. **But What about All the Presuppositions We've Been Taught? Like Isn't the Millennium a Thousand Years Long?** 51
   Symbolism: A Long Period of Time
5. **How about Satan? Wasn't He Supposed to Be Bound during the Millennium, and Therefore Totally Powerless?** 52
   Limited Restriction: "Not [to] Deceive the [Gentile] Nations Any Longer"
6. **What about the Tribulation?** 54
   The Fall of Jerusalem
7. **And the Antichrist? Is He the "Beast" of Revelation?** 57
   Nero
8. **But We've Always Been Taught That the Millennium Is to Be a Utopia. Isn't This True?** 59
   Satan's Limited Binding; Old Testament Prophecy: Confounding of Eternity and Church Blessings; the True Israel: the Church
9. **Aren't There Supposed to Be Signs Announcing the Coming of the Millennial Kingdom?** 63
   Christ's Person and Works
10. **What about All the Signs in Matthew 24?** 65
    Interpretation of Apocalyptic Language; the Context of the Queries and Answers in the Olivet Discourse; the End of the Jewish Age: Fall of Jerusalem
11. **What about the Last Days? Don't They Have Signs?** 70
    The New Testament Age
12. **How Do Daniel's 70 Weeks of Years Fit into Eschatology?** 73
    Heptads, Sabbatic Years, Messiah's Visitation and Mission
13. **What Does the Abomination of Desolation Mean?** 76
    Historical Incidents; Defilement of the Holy; "Veil Rent in Twain"

14. **What Is the Book of Revelation All about?** 78
    The Things Which *Were;* the Things Which *Are;*
    the Things Which *Shall Be Shortly*
15. **But What about All the Details of Revelation?** 82
    The 24 Elders; the 144,000; the Two Witnesses;
    Armageddon; the Ten Horns of the Beast;
    Gog and Magog
16. **Isn't There a Difference between the
    Day of the Lord and the Day of Christ?** 86
    Cross-Analysis of Terminology
17. **What Is in Store for the Future
    According to Amillennialism?** 88
    "Jewish Problem"; Comparative Diagrams
18. **Where Did the Whole System of
    Premillennialism Come from?** 92
    First and Second Resurrections; First and
    Second Judgments
19. **Isn't All This Just Academic? Or Does It
    Really Make a Difference in Everyday Life
    Which View We Adopt?** 95
    Inner Attitude; Heresy
20. **How about a Definition? What Are the Main
    Features Which Characterize Amillennialism?** 99
    Nature and Chronology of the Kingdom of Christ

Concluding Remarks 102
Bibliography 105
Glossary 111
Index of Names 113
Index of Scripture 115

PART ONE

AN INTRODUCTION TO AMILLENNIAL INTERPRETATION

Why a Book on Amillennialism for Lay Persons?

We are lay persons who have been taught the doctrines of premillennialism[1] since childhood, but who began struggling with the concept upon reading the Bible as rational adults. Having no alternative offered us, we accepted it, but not without much confusion and a deep yearning for more understanding. After having been introduced to amillennialism[2] and after years of study on both sides of the issue, we have come to embrace the preterist view[3] with a great deal of enthusiasm and now want to share what we've learned.

Many eminent Bible scholars with strings of credits perhaps more appropriate to theological study have written books on eschatology,[4] but often their writings are aimed at the academic level of their peers, so much so that lay people have a problem understanding. On the other hand, if there are any books for the laity on this topic, they have sometimes been so fanciful as to be categorized with *Alice in Wonderland* (e.g., Hal Lindsey's *The Late Great Planet Earth*). Furthermore, these latter have almost without exception espoused the dispensational[5] stand. It is our goal, therefore, as lay theologians to share this doctrine of amillennialism with you, our lay brothers and sisters in the Lord, in such a way that you too might have another viewpoint for serious consideration, a way to go other than premillennialism.

1. Premillennialism is the teaching that the "millennium" of Rev. 20 is a physical, utopian kingdom to be established at the end of this age for a thousand years upon the earth. This and other perhaps unfamiliar terms can be found with explanation in the Glossary, pp. 111, 112.
2. Amillennialism is the belief that the "millennium" is a spiritual kingdom with us now.
3. Preterism is a branch of amillennialism which holds that most prophecies concerning national Israel already have been fulfilled in the church as the true, spiritual Israel.
4. Eschatology means the study of last things or of the end times.
5. Dispensationalism compartmentalizes God's plan throughout history, generally futurist (i.e., kingdom prophecies have yet to be fulfilled).

We have been overwhelmed by the immensity of this topic. The ramifications of "realized"[6] eschatology to the rest of biblical interpretation are astounding, but marvelous. We've not merely studied this teaching, but we've experienced its impact on our lives and feel as though we've been transformed from perplexed dreamers vaguely anticipating all kinds of weird events, both horrible and glorious, into enthusiastic citizens of a dynamic spiritual kingdom, the church militant (as Augustine put it long ago) ruling and reigning with King Jesus today. Amillennialism is less a doctrine of the end times than of the here and now. In fact, if it concerned only a far-off future, we'd not be nearly so excited. We hope others of the Christian community might catch this vision of the present reality of the kingdom of Jesus Christ.

Jesus is indeed the ruler of the kings on the earth, as John puts it in Revelation 1:5. William Barclay asserts, "The Risen Christ is ruler of the kings of the earth in virtue of His Cross and in virtue of His rising again, for it was when He was lifted up on His Cross that He drew all men unto Him (John 12:32)" *(The Revelation of John,* 1:41).

The Proposition of This Book

The kingdom of God during the church age is the so-called millennium spoken of in Revelation 20. This is likely a new notion for most of you, but we hope to study it with you and to prove by Scripture (in context) that Jesus received a kingdom from the Father upon ascending to Heaven (Dan. 7:13-14). That kingdom is the church.

Christians today haven't seen this fulfillment of Jesus' kingship for the same reason that, in our Lord's time, the Jews failed to recognize their Messiah: a presupposition gets in the way. Israel assumed Jesus would be a political leader who would bring in a marvelous physical empire by conquering her earthly foes with divine intervention. As George Ladd puts it, "Jesus did not present Himself to Israel as the Davidic king, *as Israel interpreted that kingship.* He was king, indeed" *(Crucial Questions,* p. 114). We look back with wagging heads at their willful ignor-

---

6. The adjective "realized" (or "accomplished," "fulfilled") renders the concept of eschatology to be contemporary.

ance, but who are we to judge them, seeing all the hindsight we have in the New Testament, especially since so many of us are making the same blind error! We are looking for such a king, as well, one who will reign some day in geographical Jerusalem with physical power and material glory. As if the kingdom He's already made of us isn't good enough! Haven't we learned a lesson from the ancient Jews? Apparently not.

The kingdom of God has existed since creation, and it has never been (nor will it ever be) anything other than a *spiritual* kingdom, not limited to one generation or geography. This idea is probably not new to you; it is acceptable theology even to premillenarians. However, it is our intention to show that this incorporeal kingdom of God's people about the face of the earth has come under the rule of the Son during the New Testament age (including the present) and hence is one and the same as the "thousand year" reign where Satan is "bound" in a way unique to the age immediately following the victory of the cross.

The kingdom of God from creation until the New Testament was under the direct rule of the Father, but in His divine plan He handed this nonphysical domain over to the Son when the latter ascended into His presence (Matt. 28:18; Rev. 1:5-6; 5:10). Then, at the end of the present gospel age, the Son will return the kingdom (a bride "without spot or wrinkle," Eph. 5:27) to His Father for eternity future (I Cor. 15:24-25). If there are any so-called "dispensations"[7] at all, they are these three: the Father's rule in the Old Testament age, the Son's reign in the New Testament age (when Jesus reconciles the elect), and finally the Father's reinstatement at the end of time as we know it, forever and ever. Admittedly, this sounds like an over-simplification of a colossal program, but theology, like all philosophy, relies on symbols so it can be understood.

H. L. Payne has enumerated the main features of the amillennial view of Christ's kingdom: "1. The kingdom is heavenly rather than earthly. 2. It is spiritual rather than political. 3. It is present rather than future. 4. Its point of inauguration is the first rather than the second advent. 5. Its king is in heaven rather than in Jerusalem. 6. Its subjects are found in the church of God rather than the nation Israel" (*Amillennial Theology as a System*, pp. 21-22).

---

7. Dispensations are periods of time when planned changes occur in God's "economy," or program.

This is in essence our proposition. We trust we can demonstrate to your satisfaction that it is based on a thorough study of God's record. Though it may be a new thought for you, please bear with us. You'll see a marvelous overview of God's plan in history, a clearer interpretation of both the present and future ages, and a far simpler (but not simplistic) understanding of some of the more obscure, encumbered passages in the highly imagistic books of the Bible, like Daniel and Revelation.

Some of you may ask a few initial questions, such as, What of the thousand years? or, What about the utopian nature of the millennium? or, Isn't Satan bound during the age the way we've been taught? How about the great tribulation? Isn't the millennium a physical kingdom to be set up in geographical Jerusalem? We'll get to these questions and others one by one, but first let's take a brief look at the concept of interpretation, then at the history of this doctrine called *amillennialism*.

Principles of Interpretation

In response to arguments from those who believe that we must never *interpret* the Bible, but simply "read what's there," we would reply that every time a reader looks at Scripture (or any other book, for that matter), he changes it from written symbols into abstractions of thought. This is a form of interpretation, an integral characteristic of both reading and study. Without interpretation, we learn nothing.

Moderation between Overliteralization and "Higher Criticism"

Before anything else is said, we would emphasize our belief in the inspiration of God's Holy Word. We hold that the original manuscripts in Greek and Hebrew stand without fallacy, and that God has handed down to us translations from these first texts that adhere by the grace of God as closely to the spirit and to the letter of truth as possible. However, faith in the inerrancy of Scripture does not preclude a spiritual interpretation where the context would so indicate. In other words, our approach to biblical understanding will be literal insofar as the context warrants, but symbolic where the language itself implies such an approach was the divine intention.

The latter procedure is why literalists often accuse amillennialists of "liberalizing" the Word of God. But we would answer with George Ladd that the Bible often interprets itself figuratively: "To Dispensationalists, a 'spiritualizing' hermeneutic [method of interpretation] is the most dangerous way to interpret the Old Testament. . . . The present writer feels that he must adopt a spiritualizing hermeneutic because he *finds the New Testament applying to the spiritual church promises which in the Old Testament refer to literal Israel"* (*The Last Things*, pp. 22-23). For instance, Peter claims Joel's cosmic prophecy (Joel 2:30-31) as accomplished in his day, thereby rendering its sense nonliteral (Acts 2:19-20). So if the Scriptures and the apostles interpret concrete pictures spiritually, why should we be labeled as "liberal" in so doing, especially when the import of God's message is intensified, not diffused! We might sum up our feelings by agreeing with L. Berkhof: "The New Testament certainly does not favor the literalism of Premillenarians" (*Systematic Theology*, p. 713).

Even the Old Testament warns against literalism. It tells us that God spoke to the prophets in visions and dreams, dark sayings and parables (Num. 12; Hos. 12). The point is that we should interpret these Old Testament passages as intended: figuratively or spiritually. Furthermore, the only way the Old Testament writers could communicate their ideas was in the familiar framework of the symbols they knew: Israel, the temple, the throne of David, Jerusalem. If they had employed New Testament terminology (the church, grace) their words would have been essentially meaningless to a people attuned to the concrete nature of the Hebrew tongue.

Jesus Himself asserted that the spiritual language of the nonphysical truth was too much for the disciples to bear (John 16:12). For instance, He spoke of eating His flesh and drinking His blood (John 6:54). This offended the disciples because they were taking Him literally instead of metaphorically. And our Lord used the name Elijah in reference to John the Baptist (Mark 9:12-13), hardly meant to be taken at face value.

Accordingly, the vivid pictures of the end are not intended for "letteristic" interpretation, but figurative—keeping with scriptural precedent. Indeed, a hyperliteral approach to biblical understanding can be as dangerous as the rationalistic. The former can lead us away from the message of the passage in question because it bogs us down too much in the isolated meaning of each and every word. If we miss the point, what good is each word? ("For the letter killeth, but the spirit giveth life," II Cor. 3:6, Authorized Version). Or, to paraphrase a cliché, we can't see the forest because the trees get in the way. Sometimes overliteralization can even lead to scriptural contradiction, especially if a verse is taken out of context (e.g., cf. Luke 17:20 and Luke 21:31). And whereas amillennialists have been made bedfellows with liberals,[8] the reply could be that premillennialists are bedfellows of the cults, since the latter (besides being strongly dispensational) tend toward noncontextual hyperliteralization.

Likewise, modernists would have us apply their "higher criticism" or "reason" to biblical interpretation. We're surely not against rational thought, but such a philosophy as a whole can water down even the clearest teaching and thereby spiritualize away the very core of meaning in a Bible passage. Either extreme ("letteristic" or rationalistic) renders us the losers if we miss what God wanted us to heed.

The Contextual Method

How do we know which way to go? The text itself gives the required clues. Is it doctrinal or visionary? Are the words imagistic or prosaic? Or is the passage simply a narrative? Is the thrust or mood of the book a mysterious code, or is it direct? Does the Bible interpret the text elsewhere or not? It may sound confusing, but it really isn't. Scripture lets us know. And we should be consistent, too. For example, in his *Exposition of Revelation,* Walter Scott would have us interpret the "key" and the "chain" of Revelation 20:1 symbolically (and rightly so), but denies that the 1000 years of the following verses should be taken the same way. Surely it is clear that the entire passage was meant to be figurative, not just some of it.

All in all, then, we seek to take a moderate approach, one that is "natural," whereby we take the Word of God literally when we can and when we think the context would indicate that God so intended, but

---

8. Cf. Feinberg's *Millennialism: The Two Major Views.*

whereby we may construe some of the more metaphorical language with a spiritual methodology. As mentioned above, this will be the case especially in the highly imagistic writings, where we have elaborate visions and terrifically symbolic words, each representing the conceptual substance of truth; these books are most likely apocalyptic,[9] such as Daniel, Ezekiel, and Revelation. By polarizing in neither direction, we hope to comprehend God's express meaning about prophecy and eschatology.

It might be good to reiterate at this juncture that amillennialism is actually a system of theology which embraces *all* of the "last days" (Acts 2), from the New Testament era right through to the Lord's return. Hence, it concerns itself with today just as much as (if not more than) the future. William (Ed) Cox concurs; he sees the millennium as "the period of time between the two advents of our Lord, that is, as going on at the present time and ending when our Lord returns" (*Biblical Studies in Final Things,* p. 179). And God's kingdom is broader than that: it's actually a timeless entity.

The New Testament Interprets the Old Testament

Remember, wherever we deal with Old Testament prophecy in this study, we will be interpreting it in light of the more complete revelation of the New Testament. This approach is necessary because the Old Testament alone constitutes a Jewish document. With the addition of the New Testament, it becomes a Christian document. In quoting Charles Hodge, Hoekema gives an excellent argument for such a procedure: "Hodge notes that, though many prophecies are given by the Old Testament prophets about the First Advent of Christ, no one knew exactly how those prophecies would be fulfilled until Christ had actually come: 'Christ was indeed a king, but no such king as the world had ever seen, and such as no man expected; He was a priest, but the only priest that ever lived of whose priesthood He was Himself the victim; He did establish a kingdom, but it was not of this world' " (A. Hoekema, *The Bible and the Future,* p. 132; C. Hodge, *Systematic Theology,* 3:790).

9. Apocalyptic literature is full of images signifying mysteries which involve supernatural holocaust and generally denote the end of an age, not necessarily the end of all time.

Therefore, without the New Testament, the Old Testament prophecies not only lie in mystery, but are incomplete as well.

Even the New Testament writers apply Old Testament predictions to fulfillment in their own day, thereby accomplishing the intended prophetic meaning, which would have remained incomplete without the New Testament claims. In Acts 15:13-18, James quotes Amos 9:11-12 in reference to the ingathering of the Gentiles as "a people for His name." Matthew states in his Gospel (chap. 21) that Zechariah 9:9 was realized when Jesus entered Jerusalem as a king on a donkey. In the second chapter of Acts, Peter applies Joel 2:28-32 to the outpouring of the Holy Spirit on Pentecost in Bible times. In the same sermon (Acts 2:30-31), Peter says we don't need to await a distant millennial age for Jesus to sit on the throne of David since it's already done, referring directly to Psalm 16:8-11 and II Samuel 7:12. The apostle Paul claims Hosea's words (2:23 and 1:10) as fulfilled in the New Testament church (Rom. 9:24-26). And in Galatians 3:8, Paul says that the promise made to Abraham's seed (Gen. 18:18) has come to pass in God's justification of the Gentiles by their faith in Him. These are only a few of the many New Testament texts where direct reference to Old Testament prophecy is made and where fulfillment is claimed for that day.[10]

The Bible need not be a maze of incomprehensible words and phrases. Confusion is exactly what we have, though, when we allow each news story the media present to alter our interpretation of prophecy. Almost every generation that comes along sees fulfillment of prophecies that have in fact been accomplished during the Bible era. Never should Scripture be understood in light of the many vicissitudes of current events, but rather the Word of God is the standard by which history ought to be interpreted. The amillennial approach to the study of "final things" should help us do just that.

---

10. Cf. Tasker's *Old Testament in the New Testament* for a fuller discussion on this issue.

PART II

THE HISTORICAL AUTHENTICITY OF AMILLENNIALISM

Preliminary Remarks

Lest any of you think that this teaching is a Johnny-come-lately doctrine, let us state unequivocally that it belongs to the faith of our fathers. The word "amillennialism" may be relatively new, but the theology itself is ancient. And whereas dispensational premillennialism appears to be the predominant eschatological doctrine these days among fundamental denominations, it is actually as young as 1830. It developed at that time as an outgrowth of a more established premillennial system called *historical* or *classical* premillennialism, of which there are followers today. In earlier times, it was known as *chiliasm* or simply *millenarianism* (millennialism) and is admittedly as old as the first century. (In fact, we will see later on that it is based on an even more ancient Jewish misconception of God's kingdom.) Amillennial thought has existed since the first century too, but if it is truth as we contend, then it is as "old" as Scripture itself. Thus, the two systems (classical premillennialism and amillennialism) have grown up together from earliest days, two schools of theology side by side, even as they are today.

The Distinction between Classical and Dispensational Premillennialism

By way of parenthesis, we should insert here some explanatory information concerning the principal difference between dispensational and classical premillennialism. It lies in their respective views of the church/kingdom. The former calls this present age of the church the "mystery kingdom"[1] (or "great parenthesis"[2]), which its adherents

---

1. So called because the apostle Paul speaks of a "mystery" in a few of his letters (Rom. 11:25; Eph. 1:9; Col. 2:2, etc., several "mysteries" involved, all pertaining to the present age). These "mysteries" revealed to Paul were actually spelled out in the Old

insist was not prophesied in the Old Testament, while the latter agrees with amillennialism that the church is "true Israel," fulfilling the Old Testament prophecies that dispensationalists ascribe wholly to a future millennium. However, classical premillennialists contend that the church is only an "inaugurated" kingdom to be "consummated" in a physical millennium yet future. On the other hand, the amillennialist is persuaded that the spiritual kingdom which Christians presently comprise is one and the same as the messianic kingdom promised in the Old Testament; it is the church (the millennium) to be terminated at the second advent and superseded by the Father's eternal dominion.

Whatever we call the futurist view (classical or dispensational premillennialism), it encompasses the idea of a physical reign of Jesus Christ on earth at the end of the church age. Some have called chiliast eschatology "Judaized" (or even "Zionist") Christianity, because it stems from the Jewish "two-age" belief that God would vindicate national Israel (despite her disobedience) out of the present evil age by establishing her as a powerful government in a future period of indescribable earthly splendor. (It is precisely because of this fanatic conviction that the Jews rejected Jesus as their Messiah!)

Contrary to what you might have been taught, premillennialism is no more orthodox than amillennial theology. By this we mean that premillennialism was not the exclusively accepted doctrine of the traditional Christian church down through the ages; indeed, it is not even the

Testament, especially as regards the Gentile role in the kingdom (Isa. 11:10; Mic. 4:2; Zech. 2:11, etc.). To disclaim prophetic reference to the kingdom of Christ (the church) is contrary to apostolic teaching. Rom. 1:1-2 asserts without doubt that the "gospel of God" was promised in the Old Testament, and verse 9 affirms that Paul was even then preaching this same gospel; hence, the present reality of Old Testament prophecy regarding the gospel, which all must agree is preached during the church age. In fact, the early Authorized Version (King James) captions many Old Testament chapters with "the church" (e.g., Isa. 30, "God's mercy to the church"; Jer. 31, "Amplitude of the church"; Mic. 4, "Glory of the church"; and so forth). Interesting, too, that some extreme dispensationalists will go so far as to claim that Jesus was in fact prepared to offer Israel a physical kingdom during His "visitation" (the first advent, or Jesus' temporal stay on earth), but because of Jewish unbelief He actually changed His mind about the eternal plan and postponed this corporeal reign until the end of the church age, which is thereby rendered no more than an afterthought! Carrying this idea through to its logical conclusion, one would have to believe that the crucifixion was also an afterthought, since it was the result of and the mark of Jewish rejection.

2. For comment on the origin of this name, please see the discussion on Daniel's 70 weeks of years, beginning on page 73.

generally accepted doctrine. It is perhaps true that since the mid-1800s it has been popularized by theologians like Scofield, Darby, Pentecost, and a host of other evangelists and pastors, but they are by no means the only Bible scholars among conservative evangelicals; they have simply been the most vociferous about their futurist beliefs, partly the fault of the amillennialist for not sharing enough, but more because dispensational eschatology is forever changing according to (and thus kept alive by) the daily news. This is why Augustine, an amillennialist, is still valid for today: his theology works the other way around by interpreting history with the never-changing Word of God. Forms of realized eschatology were held by the Reformers (John Calvin, Martin Luther, John Knox, etc.) and hark back to early-century Christians like Polycarp, Ignatius, and Origen. In point of fact, amillennialism is the historic *Christian* teaching, whereas premillennialism has adopted the historic *Judaic* teaching.

As mentioned earlier, although premillennialism has infiltrated almost every denomination, it is held by a minority of Christians. Furthermore, no major denomination teaches two resurrections or two judgments as explicit doctrine, even though such a tenet is essential to the belief in an intervening kingdom (the millennium). What is most enlightening is that none of the historic confessions of the Christian faith contain any hint of a future reign of Christ on earth.

Most theologians, even millennially oriented, admit to these facts. Loraine Boettner agrees and puts it succinctly: "The earlier forms of premillennialism as well as the present dispensational doctrines have been held usually, if not always, by a minority of Christian people. The distinctive dispensational doctrines occupy a much less prominent place in European than in American church life" (*The Millennium*, p. 8).

Ed Cox's experience is not atypical. Having been raised on the *Scofield Reference Bible,* he struggled with the futurist doctrines therein. "Finally," he writes, "I went to the dean of the seminary and told him of my consternation. He smiled, then made a statement which I since have verified through much research. He stated that while the school of thought with which I had broken was by far the most vocal, thus giving the appearance of representing the majority opinion, actually it has always represented only a small minority of Christian thinkers. So that, rather than making a great discovery, I had merely gotten into step with the apostles, many of the church fathers, most, if not all, of the Protestant reformers, most recognized Bible commentaries, as well as most present-day teachers and writers" (William E. Cox, *Biblical Studies in Final Things*, p. 208).

But we're getting ahead of ourselves. Having touched upon the highlights above, let's start back at the beginning in more detail. As we trace the development of this one doctrine (eschatology), we will endeavor to remain as chronological as possible, so that you might have a clearer picture of the influences and circumstances that shaped its growth throughout the history of God's people.

A Look at History

The Old Testament: Up to 400 B.C.

Even during Old Testament days, the prophecies varied from a spiritual understanding in earliest times to a rather materialistic one later on. We've already cited God's promise to Abraham in Genesis 18:18 (and Gal. 3:8) as an example of the former. Yet by the time we get into some of the minor prophets, we see a distinctively Zionist polemic shaping the Jewish hope. (Zech. 14 is a good illustration of a material concept of God's kingdom.) This is not to imply that God changed His mind and spoke new thoughts to these later prophets, but rather that the mortal agent picked up influences of the time in which he lived. Nevertheless, though the Bible student can sense the human writer's Zionist bent, God kept the actual prophecies true in both word and message, which in fact have either been fulfilled spiritually in the church or will be accomplished in eternity.

All this is by way of demonstrating that even in the Old Testament there were two streams of interpretation regarding God's plan for His people. Some saw God's kingdom as righteousness triumphing over iniquity in general, and more specifically as God's elect (no matter what race) ruling over the sinful world about them through the spiritual intervention of God, by His empowering true Israel with the ability and will to do justice by faith in Him (Isa. 53; Ezek. 18; Dan. 2). On the other hand, some saw it as an unequivocal victory for the Jewish nation over all other, gentile empires (Hab. 3; Mic. 1; Joel 3), where the world would be ruled from Jerusalem upon the supernatural intervention of God, seating the Messiah on the very throne King David at one time occupied.

Let's not forget that such a literal rendering of the divine course of history was by no means universal among Old Testament writers and their contemporaries. Isaiah and Daniel, Ezekiel and Jeremiah, among others, saw beyond national Israel; they envisioned a multi-racial people of God whose hearts are sanctified by faith. "I will also make You [Messiah] a light of the nations so that My salvation may reach to the end of the earth" (Isa. 49:6). Also, "I shall give them one heart, and shall put a new spirit within them. And I shall take the heart of stone out of their flesh and give them a heart of flesh, that they may walk in My statutes and keep My ordinances, and do them. Then they will be My people, and I shall be their God" (Ezek. 11:19-20). This was a promise made to the Jewish exiles scattered among the nations. Like Jeremiah (see chap. 29), Ezekiel envisioned a new spiritual covenant replacing the former, an inferior agreement which was predicated on Israel's obedience (cf. Jer. 31:31-34 and Heb. 8:8-12).

The Intertestamental Period: 400 B.C. to Christ

Therefore, this *two-age doctrine* (Israel's present bondage, Israel's future glory) was popular from earliest days. It eventually led to what is known as apocalyptic literature, to which we referred previously. It was a particularly zealous form of Jewish writing that foresaw catastrophe for the gentile nations brought about by divine hand for the purpose of raising up a world-conquering Israelite state. On the whole, this kind of literature was not only politically chauvinistic (as though Israel had an "inside line" to Jehovah, who would vindicate His chosen people solely on the basis of race with no consideration given to their heart), but it was also highly figurative, full of visions and dreams, of horrors and delights sometimes beyond human comprehension. It was an especially popular type of writing between the testaments, during which period Israel was near her lowest ebb ever, both nationally and spiritually. Apocalyptic literature was the product of an indefatigable Zionist hope, cherished for centuries, demanding literal fulfillment.

The ideas regarding a utopian kingdom of God on earth expressed in these unique works are the early foundation for premillennialism among some Christian groups, as well as among most of the more established cults. If this Jewish interpretation of God's plan is correct, then the theological system arising out of it is too—and vice versa. But God Himself has shown us that such a view is incorrect. By rejecting Jesus' spiritual messiahship in favor of a physical reign, the Jews forfeited the kingdom of God to the Gentiles, all part of God's original program (Deut. 29:4; Ps. 95:10; Matt. 21:43; Acts 2:23; Rom. 11:11).

During these years (400 B.C. to Messiah), there was a wide variety of interpretation concerning the details of the messianic reign. The ancient rabbis had extremely lively debates in this regard: How great would be the physical luxury? How extensive the political power? But mostly, how long would it be? At first it was to be an eternal kingdom, but with changing political conditions a time limitation was eventually set. It varied from 40 years to 100 to 400 to 600 to 1000 to 2000 to 7000, depending on the opinion. The most common thinking held to the number 1000, based on Psalm 90:4, where a thousand years is to God as yesterday; this idea was reiterated later in II Peter 3:8. Such a concept, combined with the seven-day creation account, led the Jews to believe that God's "day of rest" would be the seventh day, or 1000 years long. In all these cases, the millennium was definitely a materialistic kingdom.

Some of the intertestamental Jewish apocalypses were I Enoch, Jubilees, Book of Adam and Eve, and the Syballine Oracles. Like these, Samaritan literature also expressed a belief that their Messiah (called Taheb) would reign for a certain period of years. These earlier apocalypses certainly influenced many Jewish writers during the New Testament era to continue with the traditional doctrine. II Enoch, Baruch, and IV Ezra reflect this trend.

The New Testament

Since the millennium is taught explicitly nowhere in the New Testament except Revelation 20, we have to ask ourselves about its source. This two-age belief described above provides the answer: it is really not a Christian teaching. Both William Barclay and J. M. Ford contend that the Revelation is of primarily Jewish origin. Referring to the twentieth chapter, Barclay writes, ". . . its whole background is, in fact, Jewish and not Christian" (*The Revelation of John,* 2:244). And Ford: "The verses 20:4-6 are primarily of Jewish origin not Christian" (*Revelation,* p. 354). Once again, this is not to say that the last book of the Bible lacks full status as inspired Scripture, but only that the human writer applied the imagery of apocalyptic literature to a Christian message.

This is the background that shaped the thinking of even our beloved New Testament writers. They were Jews, probably highly imbued with such a hope. This is how Latourette sees it: "From the records, we can be confident that Jesus refused to fit into any of the stereotypes which contemporaries had of the Messiah. He had come to the conviction that the mission given Him by His Father differed basically from the popular conceptions—even those held by His immediate disciples" (*Christianity Through the Ages,* p. 28).

In fact, our Lord apparently had to straighten out their understanding in this regard on many occasions. Again and again He reminded the disciples that the kingdom He was to establish would be taken from the Jews and given to the Gentiles (Matt. 21:43; Luke 13:35), but the people persisted in their misconception. Concerning the reinstatement of a Jewish polity, He reiterated the unique nature and actual presence of this kingdom He was ushering in: it had "come near" (Luke 10:9), it was already "at hand" (Matt. 3:2; Mark 1:15, etc.), it had "come upon them" (Luke 11:20), it was even then "in their midst" (Luke 17:21), it was not to be "of this world" (John 18:36).

Note that Jesus lays no claim to a temporal government in Jerusalem for any period of time—either in His own day, or any subsequent to it. Back in 1843, Richard Whateley, the archbishop of Dublin at the time, published a couple of essays wherein he takes a very strong stand on this issue. He asserts that if Jesus had in the back of His mind that someday in the future His kingdom would be earthly, a deception is before us. He writes,

> Jesus then it is plain, when He said "My kingdom is not of this world" could not have meant to be *understood* as implying that it *should* be so hereafter. . . . But had He then some *hidden* meaning, which He did *not* intend to be understood at the time? Did He design to convey one sense to the Roman governor, and another to his own disciples?—to reserve for his followers in future times, that . . . which He *pretended* to disclaim. . . . It might seem

incredible . . . that persons professing a deep reverence for Christ and his Apostles . . . should attribute to them this double-dealing; . . . if I could believe Jesus to have been guilty of such subterfuges as I have been speaking of, I not only could not acknowledge Him as sent from God, but should reject Him with *the deepest moral indignation (The Kingdom of Christ,* pp. 36, 37, 38, 40, 41).

Moreover, Jesus warned of the destruction of the temple and of the devastation that would befall Jerusalem in A.D. 70, but they comprehended not. The author of an obscure volume published in 1882 and entitled *The Fall of Jerusalem* put it this way:

> It was while gazing on this magnificent city that our Lord delivered his solemn prophecy of its approaching downfall. His disciples, their hearts burning with patriotic fervour, not unnaturally began to praise its exceeding beauty, and especially to dwell with fond affection on the superb character of its Temple,—"how it was adorned with goodly stones and gifts." . . . But he, piercing the clouds which obscured the human view, dispelled in a moment all their visions, and overwhelmed with sorrow their boastful minds. "As for these things which ye behold," he exclaimed, "the days will come in the which there shall not be left one stone upon another, that shall not be thrown down." We can imagine the consternation with which the disciples listened to this terrible prediction . . . (pp. 15-16).

The writer of this little book himself has interpreted the fall of Jerusalem from a preterist viewpoint: "We are impressed by the fact that the downfall of the Holy City was the fulfilment of a distinct prophecy, and the last unmistakable sign that the old order had changed, giving place to the new—that the Old Dispensation had passed away, to be succeeded by the religion of Christ" (Preface, *The Fall of Jerusalem*).

But the disciples didn't perceive it this way, despite Jesus' clear descriptions—not until Titus' legions actually surrounded Jerusalem, when they remembered and obeyed. As Ellen White describes it: "Not one Christian perished in the destruction of Jerusalem. Christ had given His disciples warning, and all who believed His words watched for the promised sign. 'When ye shall see Jerusalem compassed with armies,' said Jesus, 'then know that the desolation thereof is nigh. Then let them which are in Judea flee to the mountains; and let them which are in the midst of it depart out,' Luke 21:20, 21" (*The Great Controversy,* p. 30).

And so it was that even the apostles persisted in the wrong idea, as late as the first chapter of Acts. They asked Jesus before the ascension about "restoring the kingdom to Israel" (1:6), and He replied that it wasn't for them to know the times that the Father had fixed,[3] but He hinted once more at the nature of His true kingdom by making reference to Pentecost, when the Holy Spirit would empower them to spread the gospel of the kingdom "even to the remotest part of the earth" (1:8). Thus the early apostolic misunderstandings about the messianic kingdom have persisted in some circles even to this day, leading to the same misconceptions about the millennium (synonymous with the messianic kingdom).

At any rate, apparently the disciples finally got the idea! By the time Peter delivered his magnificent sermon on the day of Pentecost "not many days" (Acts 1:5) after the ascension, this Jewish apostle who so yearned for a powerful Israelite nation knew that the kingdom Jesus taught wasn't limited to the Jew and that it was already established. He claimed that the Christ was even then on the throne of David. Be sure to read Acts 2:22-36; it is proof positive that Peter no longer understood the messianic reign to be apocalyptic, as the two-age literature taught. He saw the kingdom not as physical but as spiritual, not as future but as already begun; the throne of David wasn't in geographical Jerusalem, but was occupied by Jesus in heaven.

And the apostle Paul, a Jew so zealous for Israel that he gladly slaughtered Christians before his conversion because of their threat to the Hebrew religion and state, certainly perceived the spiritual fulfillment of God's promises to His "chosen people," the elect. "For He [the Father] delivered us from the domain of darkness, and transferred us to the kingdom of His beloved Son" (Col. 1:13). "And you brethren [Gentiles], like Isaac, are children of promise" (Gal. 4:28, especially in context: 21-31). And Romans 9:6, "For they are not all Israel who are descended from Israel." (Also Rom. 2:28-29.) Paul was the apostle to the Gentiles; he even called himself that in Romans 11:13. He surely knew that the kingdom of true Israel was indeed a chosen people, persons of all races about the earth who are righteous by faith in Him who died for them and who was on the throne, ruling and reigning not only in individual lives, but above His worldwide nation.

Neither can there be any doubt about the stand the other New Testa-

---

3. By this, Jesus cautions us not to be dogmatic while probing with theological calculators into realms not revealed in the Word of God.

ment writers took. John the divine called Jesus "the ruler of the kings of the earth" (Rev. 1:5) and asserted that our Lord "has made us [the gentile churches to whom he was addressing his letters, as well as himself, almost certainly a Jew] to be a kingdom" (Rev. 1:6). John called himself a "fellow partaker in the tribulation and kingdom" (Rev. 1:9), so he evidently believed Christ's dominion was present even as he wrote.

The writer of the Epistle to the Hebrews had one of the most profound understandings of God's eternal plan: the Old Testament sacrifices demanded of the chosen Israelite nation were mere pictures foreshadowing the greatest event in all of time, the sacrifice through death of God incarnate and His victory over evil through the resurrection, which put an end forever to all physical sacrifice.[4] And this book was likely written to *Jews!* The author was sure to make it clear that Jesus' blood was superior to all and that he was enthroned in heaven: "Not through the blood of goats and calves, but through His own blood, He entered the holy place once for all, having obtained eternal redemption" (Heb. 9:12). We see here the picture of the true heavenly temple, not a literal temple erected by man in Jerusalem, where reestablished sacrifices yet future would be of no avail. Indeed, they would be an insult to God, since they imply that Jesus' sacrifice wasn't sufficient, heresy of the worst kind!

So it was that the New Testament writers finally got the full picture of a spiritual kingdom even then established, despite the fact that most (if not all) of them were of Jewish heritage. This would have put them in even greater contrast to the rest of Hebrew contemporary philosophy, where the rabbis were still arguing about the actual length in years of the "coming" messianic kingdom and where the more radical politico-religious party, the Zealots, continued to fight off Roman domination in the streets. Leon Bernstein relates that "They [the Zealots] did not wish to wait till God's decree, the Messianic hope of Israel, should be fulfilled, but would rather rush into the conflict with the 'pagan enemy' and hasten its realization" (*Flavius Josephus—His Times and His Critics,* pp. 27-28). These latter were, of course, fighting for a material fulfillment of God's kingdom on earth in the form of an independent Israelite nation. They, like the rabbis, had totally missed Jesus' message and accomplishment of true messiahship.

---

4. Even Old Testament sacrifice of animals was worthless without faith; the physical has its meaning in the spiritual. Cf. Isa. 1:11-13; Jer. 6:20; Mal. 1:10.

Post-Apostolic Era, Early Church Fathers: Before A.D. 325

In the early centuries of the Christian era, the church was torn from without by unrelenting persecution at the hands of Caesar, as well as by non-Christian Jews. The church soon began to experience a new kind of threat, that of heresies here, cults there, schisms and factions everywhere. Especially dangerous was syncretism, the gradual incorporation of either or both Hellenistic (Greek) and Jewish teaching into Christian doctrine. Such influence was difficult to combat, both in its subtlety and in its quantity. Irenaeus records as many as 20 varieties of Christianity in his day (c. A.D. 130 to c. 200).

The first and second centuries were what some have called the post-apostolic era; others refer to the Christian writers of this period as the apostolic fathers. These men often (but not always) followed in the Jewish interpretation that the kingdom of God would be restored to national Israel, a continuation of the Zionist hope that, as we have seen, persisted throughout the Old Testament, between the testaments, and into the New Testament. In other words, they missed the spiritual hermeneutic explored in the writings of the apostles and preferred to cling to the tradition of a physical kingdom.

The great Reformer John Calvin saw this trend, as well. Before quoting him, Heinrich Quistorp comments on the scholar's eschatology: "Calvin sees in chiliasm a deceptive fantasy by means of which Satan began to corrupt the Christian hope soon after apostolic times. 'I dismiss the notion that Satan began already in the time of Paul to ruin this hope (of the eternality of the kingdom of God). But shortly afterwards the Chiliasts (millennialists) arose who fixed and narrowed the conception of Christ's kingdom as being of a thousand years duration' " *(Calvin's Doctrine of the Last Things,* p. 158).

Self-preservation gave the early church little time to bask in philosophy. Therefore, as noted above, many of the ancient scholars were imitators of incorrect teaching; they were borrowing the old accepted fallacies instead of developing ideas based on the further enlightenment of the apostles; they were reactionary and felt unsafe about the revolutionary notions presented in the New Testament Epistles. Thus the chiliast doctrine was relatively common, but it was never universal or even general, as claimed by modern premillennialists. It was most popular among Christian communities of Jewish extraction, and it was the standard teaching among non-Christian Jewish settlements as well; the Ebionites, the Montanists, the Nazarenes, and the Cerinthians held fast to the thousand-year belief. Nevertheless, we should keep in mind that both schools of thought (chiliast and nonchiliast) enjoyed a rather wide following.

Besides fighting for her life, one of the young church's greatest drives was the hope of the immediate return of Jesus. This kind of expectation aided the persistent misconception of the messianic kingdom. It led many early believers into cultic activities. From Will Durant we read, "When chaos threatened the Empire at the close of the second century, Tertullian and others thought that the end of the world was at hand; a Syrian bishop led his flock into the desert to meet Christ halfway, and a bishop in Pontus disorganized the life of his community by announcing that Christ would return within a year" (*Caesar and Christ*, p. 603).

We ought not be too quick to scorn our Christian ancestors for this kind of activity. It stems from a basic fault still in effect today: interpreting Scripture by current events. How often have we read in recent years about sects and cults who have sold their possessions and convened on a hilltop here or in a valley there to await the rapture! But despite such post-apostolic excesses (which led some like Ignatius and Origen to yearn for martyrdom), we must remember that these early church scholars were pioneers who were blazing doctrinal trails, often marked with their own blood.

Although the ancients may not have had our light, it is certain that even the chiliasts did not believe the thousand-year physical reign of Christ was far off in the future. They expected it at any moment. Therefore, even though they entertained the same Zionist error, at least they believed in its immediacy. Thus, with the passage of decades and centuries without Christ's second advent, hope waned in this direction and turned instead to the task of preaching the gospel. Nevertheless, the church fathers to the end of the third century, at least, "reveal a tendency to yield to Judaism in substituting the idea of an external community for that of a spiritual fellowship."[5]

So we see that one of the main effects of the Judaizers upon Christian-

---

5. From Louis Berkhof, *The History of Christian Doctrines* (Grand Rapids: Baker Book House, 1937), p. 68, used by permission of the publisher.

ity was their millennial interpretation, especially in those communities more directly evolved from Jewish backgrounds. But simply labeling a Jewish doctrine as "Christian" doesn't make it Christian. This kind of fallacy is at the very root of premillennialism.

Such a problem was multiplied in the early years of the church by the lack of an established canon of Scripture, a body of sacred literature which all could agree was divinely inspired and which then could be sought as the basis for doctrine and truth in everyday living. Because of so many of the syncretistic influences mentioned above, much of the material being bandied about among the local congregations was dubious—some highly unorthodox—and had to be sifted out. By the end of the second century there did seem to be a real necessity for an organization that could have enough authority to pull Christianity together into one cohesive body.

The ancient Roman Catholic church filled this role. "Faced with the hostility of a powerful government, the church felt the need of unity; it could not safely allow itself to be divided into a hundred feeble parts by every wind of intellect, by disloyal heretics, ecstatic prophets, or brilliant sons. . . . The Church felt that its experimental youth was ending, its maturity was near; it must now define its terms and proclaim the conditions of its membership. Three difficult steps were necessary: the formation of a scriptural canon, the determination of doctrine, and the organization of authority" (Will Durant, *Caesar and Christ*, p. 616).

Before citing some millenarians of this era, we should note again with emphasis that, though their teaching varied widely, none of them believed that the messianic kingdom would be thousands of years off into the future. Both Papias and Irenaeus held an extremely materialistic, even hedonistic view of the millennium, whereas Hippolytus, Nepos, and Methodius were less so. Hermas and Tertullian were definitely nonextravagant in their chiliast descriptions. Justin Martyr spoke of nonchiliasts as "pure Christians," and he neither condoned nor condemned them and their stand. Although he is claimed fervently by premillennialists as an early example of their thinking, this second-century scholar believed in only one resurrection and one judgment, albeit his opinions are at times inconsistent. This is a highly unusual position for a premillenarian. Furthermore, Justin Martyr took true Israel to be the church, very definitely an amillennial teaching.

While many of the above were influenced by Zionist doctrine, others were not. Especially was this the case in Alexandria. The entire Alexandrian school split markedly from chiliasm and saw the allegorical implications of eschatology instead. Most noteworthy among these were Clement of Alexandria and Origen. The latter was perhaps the greatest Christian philosopher of his day; he believed firmly in a spiritual kingdom of Christ among believers of all races and times. He felt that hoping for a physical kingdom on earth was contrary to biblical emphasis on the nonmaterial. (Like many others of his day, he went to excess because he was forging the way, but his view on this subject is crystal clear, all the same.)

Dionysius of Alexandria was also nonchiliast; his rebuttal to Nepos' sensual concept of the millennium was kind. "After I had called the presbyters and teachers of the brethren in the villages," he tells us in the second of his *Promises,* "when those brethren had come who wished to be present, I exhorted them to examine the doctrine publicly. When they had produced this book [Nepos' exposition of the Revelation] as a kind of armour and impregnable fortress, I sat with them for three days, from morning till evening, attempting to refute what it contained" (recorded in Eusebius' *Ecclesiastical History*). Dionysius' arguments met with success; he asserts that the local chiliast leader by the name of Coracio "confessed and avowed to us" that he was persuaded of Nepos' error.

Not only the Alexandrian school, but the rest of the Egyptian church experienced a great deal of schism over this doctrine, as well. And elsewhere Polycarp wrote of a general judgment at the second advent, but there was not a word about a millennial kingdom on earth. Concerning Christ he writes, "To Him all things in heaven and earth are subject. Him every spirit serves. He comes as the judge of the living and the dead" (*The Epistle of Polycarp to the Philippians,* 2:1).

Clement of Rome was nonmillennial too, and Eusebius was downright contemptuous of his chiliast contemporary Papias: "I suppose he got those ideas through a misunderstanding of the apostolic records, not perceiving that the things said by them were said mystically in figures. For he seems to have been of very limited understanding." (*Ecclesiastical History,* 3:38). *The Letter of Barnabas* emphasizes the spiritual fulfillment (rather than literal) of Old Testament ritual in Jesus and the new covenant; its subject and application are similar to the New Testament book of Hebrews.

Caius of Rome, Tyconius, Theophilus, Ignatius, Tatian, Athanasius—all of these church fathers were utterly silent about a physical reign of a thousand years duration in Jerusalem. *The Didache,* an early church manual, makes no mention of an earthly millennium, either. If these were chiliast, they probably would have been outspoken like the others, since their system of theology is so intricately wrapped up in the concept. Grier puts it well: "Who ever met a pre-millenarian who could keep from mentioning it?"[6]

The earliest forms of the Apostles' Creed come out of this time period, and they contain no hint whatsoever of a corporeal kingdom of Christ. Thus we can say with Berkhof that both strains of eschatology existed in the first few centuries of the infant church, "but it is not correct to say, as Premillenarians do, that it [Chiliasm] was *generally* accepted in the first three centuries. The truth of the matter is that the adherents of this doctrine were a rather limited number."[7]

The Apologists: After A.D. 325

Following the worst Roman persecution of Christians under Diocletian (A.D. 303 to 323), the fourth and fifth centuries were relatively calm for the church. This had a great deal to do with state sanction in the wake of Constantine's conversion to Christianity in 312. Such official approval seemed like a blessing, since it gave the church scholars time to breathe and reflect without fear of reprisal, to think for themselves at last, to devise creeds of doctrine, to decide on a canon acceptable to all factions. A.D. 325 is a significant date because of the Council of Nicea, where a thousand bishops, deacons, and laymen gathered to defeat the most dangerous heresy of their day, concerning the deity of Jesus Christ. From this council has derived one of the greatest of all Christian formulations, the Nicene Creed. Like the Apostles' Creed, this statement of belief is entirely nonchiliast. Because of such accomplishments, these

---

6. W. J. Grier, *The Momentous Event* (Carlisle, Pa.: The Banner of Truth Trust, 1945), p. 22.
7. From Louis Berkhof, *The History of Christian Doctrines* (Grand Rapids: Baker Book House, 1937), p. 262, used by permission of the publisher.

early theologians have come to be known as the "apologists," defenders of the faith, you might say.

As is often the case, relaxed fear can be detrimental, too. Latourette writes, "Under Imperial favor the Church experienced a rapid growth. Many who thronged into it did so from expediency, rather than deep religious conviction, and the moral and spiritual quality of the Christian community suffered" (*Christianity Through the Ages,* p. 36).

Despite these first signs of decay that would last for centuries, there was growth away from the strict literalism that had plagued the younger church. As noted above, with Jesus' second coming not having occurred as expected, Christians turned their minds and hearts to the task at hand: spreading the gospel. Therefore, Christian doctrine included less and less eschatology in general, and more specifically chiliasm was on a definite wane, with temporary millennial revivals scattered here and there. This was also due to the fact that the Jewish influence was weakening on an increasingly gentile church. Unfortunately, writers who may have been denying Jewish literalism were clinging more and more to Greek philosophy, which tended toward over-spiritualization, an early form of liberalism. A balance had to be found.

Origen may have allegorized the millennium, but in the fourth century "Tyconius launched the spiritual interpretation of the Millennium (which was given its classic form by Augustine) . . ." (J. M. Ford, *Revelation,* pp. 350-51). Furthermore, in this same period of time Jerome was militantly anti-chiliast. He spoke derogatorily of "these half-Jews who look for a Jerusalem of gold and precious stones from heaven, and a future kingdom of a thousand years, in which all nations shall serve Israel" (*Commentaries on Isaiah,* 60:1).[8]

And so it was that during the fourth and fifth centuries millenarianism was given a near death blow. St. Ambrose, a chiliast, indirectly influenced one of his pagan converts, St. Augustine, to become *the* theologian of amillennialism. The elder urged his student to read the Bible for himself instead of relying on what his predecessors had thought

---

8. Most modern premillennialists prefer to emphasize the sacred aspects of their future physical millennium. Though many (especially dispensationalists) believe in a reestablished Judaic order in Israel, they contend that this dominion will rule the earth in righteousness, truth, and peace. However, the fact that they apply spiritual characteristics to the millennium does not validate their assumption that it will be either physical or future.

and written. By so doing, one of the greatest Bible scholars of all time began to see that there were two realms of existence or "cities," as he put it: one belonged to this world and was innately evil, while the other was named the "City of God," the title of Augustine's profound study on the kingdom of God. According to this view, two simultaneous kingdoms coexist in spite of each other; Christians may live in the world, but they are citizens of another, the kingdom of God, the messianic kingdom, the millennium. He writes, "Therefore, this man [King Saul] figuratively represented the people of Israel, which was to lose the kingdom, Christ Jesus our Lord being about to reign, not carnally, but spiritually" (*The City of God*, 17:7). And in his *De Trinitate:* "The Bible . . . need not always be taken literally; it was written to be intelligible to simple minds, and had to use corporeal terms for spiritual realities" (i, I).

The only chiliast bent Augustine retained was his belief that this reign of Christ would in fact be exactly 1000 years long, an understandable interpretation, considering that he lived during the first millennium (1000 years) of the Christian church and therefore did not have our hindsight.

Ford explains Augustine's view this way:

> Concerning the spiritual interpretation of the millennium, according to St. Augustine John [in the Revelation] adapted the imagery of the Jewish intermediate reign and eschatological combat to Christian realities. The millennium is the whole phase of the reign of Christ from the incarnation to the parousia [second advent]. During this time the influence of the devil is in abeyance. It is the Church militant, Augustine continues, that reigns with Christ until the end of the world; the first resurrection is to be understood spiritually as the birth into the life of grace (*Revelation*, p. 351).

Allis asserts that when Berkhof describes amillennialism as "the historic faith of the Christian Church, he is referring to the Augustinian view in general" (*Prophecy and the Church*, p. 6). Berkhof himself writes, "In the west the powerful influence of Augustine was instrumental in turning the thoughts of the Church from the future to the present by his identification of the Church and the Kingdom of God. He taught the people to look for the millennium in the present Christian dispensation."[9]

9. From Louis Berkhof, *The History of Christian Doctrines* (Grand Rapids : Baker Book House, 1937), p. 262-63, used by permission of the publisher.

We, too, would agree with those who have asserted that the influence of this remarkable theologian on the decline of millennialism can hardly be calculated. "Augustine, says S. J. Case, laid 'the ghost of (pre)millennialism so effectively that for centuries the subject was practically ignored.' "[10]

With Augustine's death, the shell of the Christian organization became larger and more noticeable, but it was increasingly dry and cracked, like a dropped egg. The yolk, though, the true Christian remnant, remained vital, as God has guaranteed in His Word. Nevertheless, the Roman Church strengthened the established creeds and canon, even while her hierarchy began suffering from over-bloating.

In summary, then, regarding this era Berkhof says, "It is quite evident from the writings of the Apologists that . . . their work marked the beginning of Christian theology, though this was forced into a philosophical framework."[11]

One of the ways the church formulated her theology was the practice of convening in councils for determining the soundness of doctrine. In 431 a council met in Ephesus that brought the gavel down hard and heavy against millenarianism. Ford writes, "The council at Ephesus spoke of chiliasm, the belief in the earthly reign of Christ incarnate which will usher in the millennium, as a deviation and fable. It practically died out in the Church" (*Revelation,* p. 351).

Just 20 years later, in 451, the Council at Chalcedon, near Constantinople, drew up a statement of faith that is considered by many to be one of the most widely accepted creeds in all of Christendom, second only to the Apostles' Creed and perhaps the Westminster Confession. Like all the great doctrinal documents of the Christian faith, it leaves out all reference whatsoever to any kind of millennial teaching. Indeed, there isn't even a way to squeeze chiliasm between the lines.

---

10. From W. J. Grier, *The Momentous Event* (Carlisle, Pa.: The Banner of Truth Trust, 1945),p. 27.
11. From Louis Berkhof, *The History of Christian Doctrines* (Grand Rapids: Baker Book House, 1937), p. 60, used by permission of the publisher.

The Dark (Middle) Ages: 500 to 1400

Berkhof asserts that during the next period of church history (sixth through fifteenth centuries), "millenarianism was generally regarded as heretical."[12] However, because of gross spiritual darkness at the hands of a corrupt Roman Church, there was little true doctrine being taught—of any kind. The only emphasis was on keeping the populace in ignorance by hiding the Word of God away from them. Such sin—that of sending others to hell—could hardly be more heinous! It is little wonder that many of the Reformers soon to follow called the papacy "the Antichrist." The Roman hierarchy was immoral (e.g., the clergy could pay the church for absolution from the sin of keeping concubines, while marriage remained off-limits) and unethical (e.g., "indulgences" were the way of salvation: put money into the papal coffers for forgiveness of sins), not to mention murderous (e.g., the Inquisition during the thirteenth through the fifteenth centuries).

With so little Bible teaching, eschatology was pushed further than ever into the background. However, both before and after the year 1000, it is understandable that there was a burst of revivalist fervor for the end of the world. Christ's coming was imminently expected all over again, but the thinking was not chiliast; the hopes were not aimed at a thousand-year reign of Christ on earth, but rather toward judgment and eternity. (But an Antichrist was expected to usher in the end, which would see good and evil battle each other.) Even the arts revealed and reflected fascination with the subject: paintings depicted holocaust and judgment and glory; literature was brimming with eschatological descriptions. Dante wrote his *Paradise, Inferno,* and *Divine Comedy* toward the end of this period.

In the thirteenth century, there were temporary revivals of millennialism. For instance, Joachim of Flora claimed the millennium would begin in 1260. Generally speaking, though, the Dark and Middle Ages regarded the teaching as unorthodox. Dr. Shedd indicates that during this period "millenarianism can hardly be said to have had any existence as a doctrine."[13] Even the faithful few of the increasingly pagan Roman Church were amillennial.

12. From Louis Berkhof, *The History of Christian Doctrines* (Grand Rapids: Baker Book House, 1937), p. 236, used by permission of the publisher.
13. From W. J. Grier, *The Momentous Event* (Carlisle, Pa.: The Banner of Truth Trust, 1945), p. 29.

Despite these 10 centuries of spiritual and moral decline that threatened the very life of the church, there was a remnant of true believers among the apostates. This was the glowing ember amid the cold ashes on the Roman hearth. At times it would flare up to shed light on the silt of corruption, only to be nearly extinguished by the heavy sedimentation of false doctrine.

Among the few flickering candles of the Roman Church was a movement for evangelism directed toward the common folk. Two groups which still function today grew out of this thirteenth-century crusade: the Franciscans and the Dominicans. Though a lay person, Francis of Assisi believed so strongly in sharing the gospel with the populace that he laid aside his material possessions for a spartan existence, roaming the European countryside as a friar to minister whatever way he thought God would have him go. Another ascetic, the clergyman Dominic, also was moved to be a missionary to the masses. On the heels of these godly men, Thomas Aquinas was expounding his Christian philosophy, which has come to be known as Thomism. Such evangelical fervor for the peasants and love for the Word of God were signs in the Roman Church of Christian revitalization in a generally dead era.

But these lights were too few and too far between; the corruption in the organized church had been allowed to grow for too long. It was so widespread and deep rooted that the hands of devout men were more or less forced in the direction of an all-out overhaul, the Reformation.

The Reformation: 1400 to 1550

As early as the fourteenth century, the "Morning Star of the Reformation" was speaking out in England against the evils of the Roman Church. His name was John Wycliffe (also spelled Wickliffe and Wyclyf), and he believed the populace should have the opportunity and privilege of reading the Bible; so he translated the first full version of the English Scriptures. His rendition may have been crude, but it could have introduced the Reformation into England 130 years before Luther, had Wycliffe not been censored and as much of his extant writings destroyed as could be found.

John Wycliffe may have been the first on record to label the papacy as antichrist, but he surely wasn't the last. In Bohemia, John Huss attached himself to Wycliffe's ideas. It was the early fifteenth century when he was condemned to death and burned alive. There is a fascinating story told concerning Huss' last words at the stake. According to *Fox's Book of Martyrs*, he is supposed to have said to his executioner, "You are now going to burn a goose (Huss signifying goose in the Bohemian language), but in a century you will have a swan which you can neither roast nor boil."[14]

And as though Huss were a prophet, just about 100 years later Martin Luther (whose family crest depicts a swan!) nailed his famous *Ninety-Five Theses* to the Wittenberg Door in Germany. It was 1517 when the dam burst, a dam that allowed God's Word to flood into the common man's heart, purposely parched for centuries by a debauched clergy. Like Israel's King Josiah who rediscovered God's law, Luther discovered for himself that "the just shall live by faith" (Rom. 1:17, KJV). The "indulgences" that the Roman Church was selling were abhorrent to him; that man could gain salvation by works was anathema! Sidney Ahlstrom asserts that "Luther's thought was profoundly affected by St. Augustine, the hero if not the founder of his order. . . . *Sola Gratia* [grace alone], defended so doggedly by Augustine, recurs in Aquinas, and had been affirmed by the Council of Trent (1545-63)" (*A Religious History of the American People*, p. 74).

Luther was influenced not only by Augustine's doctrine of salvation, but also by his eschatology. Like the Apologist, the Reformer firmly believed in the contemporary reign of Christ and the two coexistent kingdoms. Vajta writes that according to Luther, "God imparts his benefits to mankind through two kingdoms. In the temporal kingdom he grants earthly gifts . . . in the spiritual kingdom eternal life . . ." (*Luther on Worship*, pp. 110-11). This spiritual kingdom is the promised messianic kingdom. Furthermore, Luther held millennialism in very low regard, scorning belief in a physical dominion of God as no more than a dream. William Masselink contends that Luther held that "a millennial reign of Christ, characterized by . . . an earthly prosperity for those involved, is not to be expected by God's children in this world" (*Why Thousand Years?*, p. 279).

14. From *Fox's Book of Martyrs*, by Wm. Byron Forbush (editor); copyright 1926 by John C. Winston; copyright renewed 1954 by Holt Rinehart & Winston. Assigned to Zondervan, 1967, p. 143. Used by permission.

Indeed, so strongly did Luther reject the two-age doctrine, that he would have denied a place in the canon to Revelation because of its widespread misinterpretation. Although a nonmillennialist, Martin Luther took a "comprehensive" view of the Revelation (whence the name "comprehensivist"). In other words, he did not necessarily believe that most of the book was already fulfilled (which is the preterist position), but rather that its principles were being played out through church history.

Luther was a devout member of the Roman Catholic Church. Though repulsed by her immoral excesses, he never intended to leave her and establish another "denomination." However, of the papacy the Reformer writes, "But . . . they take from Christ His power as a heavenly Ruler, and give it to the Pope, and allow 'the form of a servant' to be entirely forgotten (Phil. ii. 7). He should properly be called the counter-Christ, whom the Scriptures call *antichrist* for his whole existence, work, and proceedings are directed against Christ, to ruin and destroy the existence and will of Christ" (*Address to the German Nobility*). Severe words for someone who never meant to abandon his denomination!

Shortly thereafter, John Calvin crystallized the Reformed doctrines in France. His *Commentaries* interpret the Antichrist as any person or group throughout history so antagonistic to the truth of the gospel as to annihilate its influence and its adherents (e.g., Islam, the pope, etc.). Also a comprehensivist, he comments concerning II Thessalonians 2:7, "The name Antichrist does not designate a single individual, but a single kingdom which extends throughout many generations."

In the "Prefatory Address" to his *Institutes,* Calvin exults more generally about Christ's kingdom:

> But our doctrine must stand . . . because it is not ours, but that of the living God and his Anointed, whom the Father has appointed King, that he may rule from sea to sea, and from the rivers even to the ends of the earth; and so rule as to smite the whole earth and its strength of iron and brass, its splendour of gold and silver, with the mere rod of his mouth, and break them in pieces like a potter's vessel; according to the magnificent predictions of the prophets respecting his kingdom (Deu. ii.34; Isaiah xi.4; Psalm ii.9) (1:6).

And further:

> The Church of Christ shall reign at the right hand of the Father. . . .

Nor ought we to doubt that Christ has always reigned on earth ever since he ascended to heaven (1:14-15).

In Switzerland there was Zwingli (who, like Luther and Calvin, was not very fond of the last book of the Bible), and in Scotland John Knox; Reformed theology was breaking out all over. Besides their emphasis on salvation by grace alone and the sovereignty of God, the Reformers were almost universally amillennial. Even Dr. John Walvoord of Dallas Theological Seminary (a stronghold of dispensational doctrine) admits this fact: "Reformed eschatology has been predominantly Amillennial. Most if not all the leaders of the Protestant Reformation were Amillennial in their eschatology, following the teachings of Augustine" (article in *Bibliotheca Sacra*, p. 111, cited by William E. Cox, *Biblical Studies in Final Things*).

Nevertheless, there were traces of chiliasm in the followers of John Huss, in Weigel and Comenius of Germany, Jurieu in France, and the Anabaptists. Some of the latter became fanatical in their attempt to erect a "New Zion" in 1534, causing the Reformers to fight the teaching all the more fervently. Bellarmine and Ribera were Jesuit priests of the sixteenth century who preached premillennialism, as well.

One of the most notable aspects of the Reformation was a profusion of councils, creeds, and confessions. If these did not actively repudiate chiliasm, they failed to mention it altogether. In 1530, the official Lutheran doctrines were spelled out in the Augsberg Confession, which condemns men "who now scatter Jewish opinions, that, before the resurrection of the dead, the godly shall occupy the kingdom of the world, the wicked being everywhere suppressed" (art. XVII). The Calvin-Zwingli branch of the Reformation drew up a document on the matter in the Second Helvetic Confession of 1536: "Moreover, we condemn the Jewish dreams, that before the day of judgment there shall be a golden age in the earth, and the godly shall possess the kingdoms of the world, their wicked enemies being trodden underfoot" (chap. XI). Between 1545 and 1563, the Council of Trent (a Roman Catholic reaction to the Protestant Reformation) collected its thoughts regarding orthodox doctrine, including eschatology; although it retained a belief in a future Antichrist, it professed a single judgment, more or less ruling out an interregnum ("in-between kingdom"). And in England the Confession of Edward VI states, "Those who attempt to revive the fable of the millenarians oppose the sacred Scriptures and throw themselves headlong into Jewish absurdities."

The Seventeenth and Eighteenth Centuries: Postmillennialism

As we move past the Reformation into the seventeenth century, we see a continuation of Reformed theology. Perhaps the most classical formulation and most widely accepted of all Christian church statements of faith is the Westminster Confession of 1647, the product of the Westminster Assembly, 1643–46. Ahlstrom comments, "That so many learned and contentious men in an age of so much theological hairsplitting could with so little coercion establish so resounding a consensus on so detailed a doctrinal statement is one of the marvels of the century" (*Religious History of America*, p. 94). The following is a portion of its thirty-third chapter, entitled "Of the Last Judgment": "God hath appointed a day wherein he will judge the world in righteousness by Jesus Christ, to whom all power and judgment is given of the Father, in which day, not only the apostate angels shall be judged, but likewise all persons, that have lived upon the earth, shall appear before the tribunal of Christ." There is no seriously honest way to fit a political reign of Christ on earth either before or after (or in the midst of) this judgment.

A few European Reformed theologians were millenarian, however, but their concept of the millennium was more spiritual. In other words, they did not believe in a visible dominion of Christ for a thousand years, but rather a nonmaterialistic kingdom on earth. They held that just before the end there would be a religious awakening such as never before. This is actually a very early form of postmillennialism, which in essence says that Jesus' return won't happen until the end of a utopia-like millennium of indeterminate duration.

While Europe may have retained such millennial thinking, the very first settlers in America were most influenced by Reformed teaching. The reason for this is quite simple, though paradoxical: the trend away from a hierarchical church system to a more congregational approach for worship was common among the discontented who fled from Europe for religious freedom in the New World. And these latter came out of the Reformation movement. However, because of their loose authoritative structure, they were more easily susceptible to doctrinal shifts. Hence, some of these "low-church" denominations were strongly influenced by the postmillennial and the dispensational movements to follow.

The eighteenth century saw a surge of popularity for postmillennialism. This system has been mistakenly viewed as totally liberal, whereas most of its early adherents were devout evangelicals who sincerely believed God was ushering in the millennium slowly but surely, to be culminated when all was perfected in a utopia on earth by the second coming of the kingdom's King, Jesus Christ. Nevertheless, there was a simultaneous growth of a more modernistic flavor within the ranks of postmillennialism. It has been called the "social gospel," characterized by a great deal of optimism and humanism (i.e., that man has the capacity for good within himself and that he will in his own strength exercise that good for the betterment of society).

The Nineteenth and Twentieth Centuries: Dispensationalism

However, Reformed theology remained the standard, right into the nineteenth century. More Protestant confessions reiterated the amillennial view of eschatology. For instance, the New Hampshire Baptist Confession of 1833 is representative of many others during this time period:

> We believe that the end of the world is approaching; that at the last day Christ will descend from heaven, and raise the dead from the grave to final retribution; that a solemn separation will then take place; that the wicked will be adjudged to endless punishment and the righteous to endless joy; and that this judgment will fix forever the final state of men in heaven or hell, on principles of righteousness (art. XVIII).

But with the increasing pessimism of a revolutionary mentality around the world, times were ripe for change. This was reflected not only in religion, but in the arts as well (e.g., a shift from the lyrical to the discordant in music, from romanticism to realism in literature, from gentle naturalism to incomprehensible surrealism in paintings, etc.). Optimistic postmillennialism, though still somewhat popular, gave way to pessimistic premillennialism. A supernatural holocaust seemed to contrast more distinctly against the bold confidence of the social gospel. Since premillennialism colored a grimmer picture of mankind and its future, it seemed to coincide more accurately with the catastrophes of current events. With this in mind, we see the inception of the modern dispensational arm of premillennialism. It began about 1830 under the leadership of J. N. Darby of the Plymouth Brethren in England. Soon its influence was felt in several European countries, but mainly in America, especially as the world entered the twentieth century and the World Wars. Many other religious teachers followed suit. Again, adherents to dispensationalism have been the more vociferous group, due at least in part to its fascinating intricacies regarding the future and to its dependence upon contemporary world news.

Premillennialists in Europe included Bengel, Oetinger, Hofmann, Delitzsch, and others, but their views differed widely at times as to order of events in their futurist schemes. It should be added here that the nineteenth century saw the beginnings of a number of the larger modern cults such as Mormonism and Jehovah's Witnesses, both of which have laid their foundations in dispensational premillennialism.

Let's not forget, though, that the historic Christian faith embraces optimistic amillennialism,[15] that is to say, a *realized spiritual* kingdom (which does not explicitly deny inherent material blessing, as well). Even Scofield admits to the historicity of this view: "Especially is it necessary to exclude the notion—a legacy in Protestant thought from post-apostolic and Roman Catholic theology—that the Church is the true Israel, and the Old Testament foreview of the kingdom is fulfilled in the Church" (*Scofield Reference Bible*, p. 989).

As we have seen, the World Wars of the twentieth century diminished the widespread following of postmillennialism, although a few scholars (e.g., L. Boettner, R. Rushdoony, and J. M. Kik) persist in evangelical circles, and in nonevangelical circles it lived on in Rauschenbusch's social gospel. Dispensationalism became extremely popular in the first half of this century, but it was never the standard position. Indeed, in the last decade or so, there has been a defection away from strict dispensationalism by some of its former adherents. Scholars have begun to

---

15. Amillennialism is the most optimistic theology because of its eschatology of victory. We will see that both premillennialism and postmillennialism postpone Christ's ultimate triumph, insofar as they look forward to a millennium.

criticize their own school's view on eschatology (George Ladd and William E. Cox, for example). Some Bible colleges are relaxing their dispensational stand, but not without reluctance. There has been a good deal of dispute even among Plymouth Brethren concerning post- and premillennialism. Nevertheless, there remain many who insist on clinging relentlessly to the fanciful precepts of dispensationalism. One of the most celebrated writers among them in recent years is Hal Lindsey.

At any rate, as Cox puts it, "Although . . . futurism has gained a wide following among many denominations, it would seem that this influence has been waning during recent decades" (*Biblical Studies in Final Things*, p. 208). You see, it takes about 150 years to test the validity and endurance of a doctrine, and dispensationalism has been found lacking. Jay Adams agrees: "Since World War II, there has been a growing concern over the secondary (and even many of the primary) tenets of the premillennial system. . . . Although dispensational premillennialism is by no means dead, and is still firmly entrenched in many of its original strongholds, there is a growing tendency to depart from its radical principles" (*The Time Is at Hand*, p. 2).

The main reason for the failure of premillennialism is that its system has misconstrued God's eternal plan and has turned scriptural priorities around. Ray Summers puts it well:

> The futurist method is associated with a materialistic philosophy of the kingdom of God and a basis of triumph for the cause of righteousness which appears to be unscriptural throughout. Any system which turns from the purposes of grace and the cross of Christ to methods of victory of any other description becomes repulsive to the sincere Christian mind. Futurism does this very thing, whether it will admit it or not. This dispensationalism is Jewish theology, largely of the apocryphal literature, and not New Testament theology.[16]

Though there was a mitigated form of premillennialism among Catholics in South America (which the Holy See quashed in 1941 and by decree in 1944), Roman Catholicism[17] has always been amillennial. The

---

16. Ray Summers, *Worthy Is the Lamb* (Nashville: Broadman Press, 1951, renewal 1979), p. 34. All rights reserved. Used by permission.

17. Following the Protestant Reformation, the godly remnant within the Roman church forced the organization to root out its evil; thus, though much of her doctrine remains unscriptural (e.g., daily repetition of Christ's sacrifice in the Mass, Mariology, penance, purgatory, etc., all of which enfeeble Christ's power as Savior), many Roman Catholics are citizens of the kingdom of God.

New American Catholic Bible footnotes Revelation 20:1-6 (regarding the thousand-year "millennium") as follows:

> Like the other numerical values in this book, *the thousand years* are not to be taken literally: they symbolize the long period of time between the chaining up of Satan (a symbol for Christ's resurrection-victory over death and the forces of evil) and the end of the world. During this time God's people share in the glorious reign of God. . . .

Orthodox Presbyterians,[18] Lutherans, the Reformed Church, Episcopalians, Eastern Orthodox—these among many retain as explicit doctrine the amillennial view of eschatology, which also finds followers in all of the other major Protestant denominations. In fact, there is a movement afoot called the Reformed American Baptists, initiated by a small group of ministers in the American Baptist Convention. This group holds more strictly to the doctrines of the Reformation in general, including amillennialism.

Furthermore, although some theologians are obviously premillenarian, they don't sound like it at times. For instance, they may write exegetically (verse-by-verse study) as though they belong to the futurist school, but when it comes to apologetics (defending doctrine in more general statements of faith), they appear to be preterist. William Barclay is a good case in point. His approach is basically premillennial: a time of horror (the tribulation) will yet appear just before the millennium, the Antichrist will make himself known at that time (duplicating Nero), Christ's reign is to be in geographical Jerusalem, when all evil will cease to hold sway, and so on. Despite this strongly futurist position, he confesses, "It will not be unfair to this doctrine [millenarianism] to say that it is a doctrine which has long since been left behind by the mainstream of Christian thought, and which now belongs rather to the eccentricities of Christian belief" (*The Revelation of John*, 2:245).

And there are other scholars who tend to be eschatologically schizophrenic in the reverse: their verse-by-verse analysis reveals them as preterists, but they sound conspicuously like futurists in their generalized "apology" or arguments. George Ladd appears to fall partially into this category. He calls himself premillennial but believes Jesus is ruling today over a kingdom, albeit a shadow of its future glory.

---

18. However, Orthodox Presbyterians understand the Westminster standards to allow for a variety of eschatological positions.

The study of the end times has never been as important as some other doctrines, and perhaps that's as it should be. Surely salvation by grace, the sovereignty of God, the deity of Jesus Christ, a sanctified life, these and other central issues upon which Christianity pivots should occupy our attention more than those peripheral areas of less significance. However, if we consider our daily life and walk and attitude as central (and we should), then in a way amillennialism isn't as peripheral as we might think. You see, by putting Jesus' kingdom way off into the unseen future, we postpone His victory; we don't fully recognize His present position at the right hand of power as Messiah-King; and we don't appreciate the wonder of this contemporary kingdom and its gifts (including the Holy Spirit). Surely these are crucial considerations. If we understood the negative repercussions of adhering to futurism, perhaps we might see that we are dealing God an insult. Eschatology—better yet, in reference to amillennialism, the study of the present-day kingdom of Christ—isn't really unimportant after all.

Perhaps in the earlier history of Christianity more time was given over to the study of the issues that threatened the very life of the church, or God's kingdom. Today, though, we can step back and learn what the nature of this once-threatened kingdom is. We would agree with Dr. James Orr that Christian dogma may have reached a sufficiently stable point where the church can now turn more attention to this particular doctrine (the character and chronology of Christ's kingdom) for further development.

PART THREE

TWENTY QUESTIONS ANSWERED

Preliminary Remarks

To preface these questions, we should say that there is not total agreement among all amillennialists as to detail on many of the issues. The one distinguishing feature of this view on which all concur is that the millennium is identical with the church age, in which we are now living and reigning with Jesus Christ in His spiritual kingdom. Furthermore, according to this position there will be no future millennium whatsoever in an earthly Jerusalem. As to topics such as the tribulation, the Antichrist, and the role the Jewish nation will play in God's future plans, there may be some latitude. However, we will be presenting primarily our own views on these matters. We're not out to substantiate any particular school of amillennial thought or any scholar we hold in especially high regard. Rather, our purpose is to discern what we believe are the truths taught in Scripture as regards the kingdom of God under the rule of Jesus Christ.

As we have said, our plan is to take you through the main issues concerning this doctrine by posing queries we think may be most troublesome to those who have been raised on premillennialism. By answering as best we can, we trust you may find a foundation of sorts for further inquiry into this thesis. The following questions represent some of the very dilemmas with which we struggled early on. Remember, it's just as difficult—if not more so—to unlearn fallacies, as it is to learn new facts.

Neither is the study of eschatology too complex (as though God were toying with us by putting us in the middle of an endless maze of confusing symbols), nor is it a childish guessing game. As Ed Cox puts it, "Eschatology often has been the plaything of undisciplined minds" (*Biblical Studies in Final Things,* p. xi). It may take some work, but it most assuredly is comprehensible.

Probably the biggest barrier to our understanding is the fear of letting go of what we've been taught, something that has come to be an endearing friend, so to speak, a rather fascinating one, we might add. As mentioned above, premillennialism appears to be the only acceptable doctrine in certain religious circles, so much so that very few hear anything else (at least for comparison), and if they do, they are informed that the alternatives are either blasphemous or heretical. Hence, the average lay person dreads the sense of aloneness that nonmillennialism (another name for amillennialism) has been known to introduce, particularly at the beginning, and especially since the adherents of premillennialism cling to it so ferociously. However, such fear should never be a deterrent to the search for truth.

Though the following answers will not cover every facet of the issues in question, they should suffice as groundwork for further study.

1. What exactly is the kingdom of God?

This is an excellent question with which to begin the discussion, because it gets down to the very root of what we're talking about. Perhaps it would be a good idea to look at the word "kingdom" linguistically. Such a study will shed light on the intent of the word and the phrase in which it appears. We could say it no better than C. H. Dodd: "The term 'kingdom' is in English somewhat ambiguous. . . . The Greek term *basileia* which it translates is also ambiguous. But there can be no doubt that the expression before us represents an Aramaic phrase well-established in Jewish usage, 'the *malkuth* of Heaven.' *Malkuth*, like other substantives of the same formation, is properly an abstract noun, meaning 'kingship,' 'kingly rule,' 'reign' or 'sovereignty.' The expression 'the *malkuth* of God' connotes the fact that God reigns as King" (*The Parables of the Kingdom,* p. 21).

Such a definition may be especially helpful to us of the Western mentality, where government is less a monarchy than a representative republic or democracy. A kingdom (incorporating the word and concept of "king") is alien to our political thinking. It is interesting that the *New American Bible* translates kingdom of God as "reign of God."

Juan Carlos Ortiz, a missionary from Argentina to the United States, focuses our attention in this direction: "The Kingdom of God means the Government of God. . . . God is the one on the top. God is the authority. . . . If you are doing your own will, you are in the Kingdom of Darkness. If you are doing God's will, you are in the Government of

God. . . . The Bible never said you have to be born again to enter into the [organized] Church—it's to get into the Kingdom. . . . A citizen of the Kingdom is a person who is under the Lordship of Christ" (transcribed from an unpublished address delivered in Redwood City, Calif., July 2, 1978).

To repeat something mentioned earlier, the kingdom of God has existed at least from creation. It is a *spiritual* kingdom, always has been, always will be. We know that Jesus claimed this fact over and over again. He said, "My kingdom is not of this world [realm]" (John 18:36). By this He did not mean that it couldn't exist among His people who still lived on earth, because he also stated that the kingdom was *among* them (the disciples) or *in their midst* (Luke 17:21). Rather, His intent was to stress that His kingdom belonged to the spiritual world, which in fact coexists with the physical world, but which is not bordered by time limitations and thus already bears characteristics of the eternal state.

When the apostle Paul writes that "flesh and blood cannot inherit the kingdom of God" (I Cor. 15:50), he isn't saying humans can't partake of God's domain while on earth, but, as he goes on to explain, that the "perishable" cannot inherit anything "imperishable." So it is that after His resurrection Jesus could say that he was not a ghost, "for a spirit does not have flesh and bones as you see that I have" (Luke 24:39). You see, what cannot inherit God's spiritual dominion is the *perishable* aspect of the flesh (a result of sin), not flesh itself. Jesus was even then in some kind of spiritual body of flesh, something we cannot now understand, but receive only by faith.

Paul also says that "the kingdom of God is not eating and drinking, but righteousness and peace and joy in the Holy Spirit" (Rom. 14:17). Once again he isn't saying we can't eat or drink in the kingdom of God, but that God's kingdom consists of more than such earthly matters; it is comprised of spiritual elements like righteousness, peace, and joy. Otherwise, Jesus wouldn't have had His facts straight when He asserted that He would some day eat and drink with us (His disciples) in God's kingdom when the Passover was fulfilled (Luke 22:16ff.). Now we know that the original Passover in Exodus 12 spoke of Israel's deliverance from the Egyptian enemy by the sprinkling of lamb's blood. In the crucifixion, Jesus fulfilled everything of which the Passover spoke. By establishing the Lord's Supper (the Eucharist), Christ replaced the Passover with the communion (meaning "fellowship"). Thus, when we partake of communion, we are fellowshipping with Jesus and supping spiritually with Him in the kingdom of God (Matt. 26:26-29).

We can, therefore, rejoice with confidence that, if we are Christians, we have already inherited Christ's kingdom of God. This kingdom is spiritual, one we enter by the new birth within the framework of the physical earth and which continues on into eternity. Heaven is God's kingdom, too. Saints beyond this life are there even at this moment. Sometimes the phrase "kingdom of God" refers in the Bible to heaven (the church triumphant), as well as to the church militant on earth. In fact, the terms kingdom of God and kingdom of heaven can be interchangeable. Matthew uses kingdom of heaven almost exclusively where the other Gospel writers use kingdom of God. Christ's kingdom today and the kingdom in heaven both belong to God's eternal, spiritual domain.

Scripture teaches that the kingdom is ours today. Jesus: "I for my part assign to you the dominion my Father assigned to me" (Luke 22:29, *New American Bible*). The writer to the Hebrews: "Therefore let us be grateful for receiving a kingdom that cannot be shaken" (Heb. 12:28, Revised Standard Version). Paul: "For our citizenship is in heaven, from which also we eagerly wait for a Savior, the Lord Jesus Christ" (Phil. 3:20). Peter: "You are a chosen race, a royal priesthood, a holy nation, a people for God's own possession, that you may proclaim the excellencies of Him who has called you out of darkness into His marvelous light" (I Pet. 2:9).

At times throughout history, some physical entities have represented this spiritual kingdom, such as King David's nation of Israel or the visible church today, but these are no more than outward appearances of the essence inside. It matters not whether a citizen of this kingdom is old or young, male or female, black or white, Jew or Gentile, from the past or the present or the future; if he has been born of God, he is a citizen of God's kingdom. And one is born of God when he gives his life over to Jesus, when he becomes a Christian.

This spiritual kingdom is more "real" than any physical domain could ever be. The most durable part of any human being is his spirit, not his body; it is everlasting (whether in heaven or in hell); it never decays. You see, incorporeality does not negate actuality; in fact, it can magnify it. The love of God is something we can't touch, but it certainly is the most significant element in a Christian's life. And so it is that such a nonmaterial realm as the kingdom of God is greater by far than any of its physical manifestations in the world. It is a superior kingdom (after all, earthly entities are but shadows, or copies, of heavenly realities, Heb. 8:2, 5), a realm where no external form of government is imposed upon us, but rather where the authority works through the very heart of man by the power of God.

So important was this proclamation of the kingdom to Jesus that He went about preaching it at nearly every turn in His ministry on earth. Surely He wasn't uttering so urgent a message, if it had no practical meaning to the people of His day; the kingdom-at-hand wasn't an event that would take place thousands of years in the future instead of during their lifetimes. By preaching the kingdom, Jesus was actually preaching salvation; they are one and the same. This was our Lord's glad tidings: the kingdom of God is a present reality and we can be a part of it if only we believe in Him. Why would any Christian today crave a physical kingdom yet to come, no matter how glorious, when he already is a citizen of an international and timeless empire such as this one that God has provided!

2. What then is the difference between the Old Testament kingdom and the New?

Although the kingdom of God has existed in both the Old and the New Testaments as the true "church" (or *ekklesia* in Greek, "the called out"; cf. Act 7:38), we will be using the outward organizations which represent these believers to illustrate a point. Earlier we mentioned King David's Israel and the visible Christian community of the structured church. The former (the Old Testament manifestation in national Israel) consisted almost exclusively of Jews, whereas the latter (the New Testament manifestation in the church institution) consists of Gentiles for the most part. Herein lies a tremendously significant distinction. During the Old Testament era, the "nations" (or Gentiles) were as a whole blinded by Satan to God's light, but in the New Testament era there was a kind of spiritual explosion of truth spread abroad to fill the earth.

Probably the main difference between the two time periods is the position held by Jesus, God the Son. In our "Proposition" at the outset of this book, we alluded to the three ages of divine rule, but it is pertinent here to repeat the idea: it was the Father who was king in the Old Testament, while in the New Testament Jesus became the ruler of the kings on the earth (Rev. 1:5). You see, it was Jehovah Father's omnipotent pleasure to hand the authority over to Jehovah the Son during this gospel phase of the kingdom of God. Therefore, uniquely, Jesus our Lord is in a very special position these present days of the church: not only is He prophet and priest, but He is also our king, the only person who could ever make claim to all three titles. Then, at the end of time, Jesus (having completed His messianic mission of reconciliation and sanctification) will return the kingdom to the Father for eternity (I Cor. 15:24).

The present-day reality of Jesus' kingship is, therefore, the most distinct feature of the New Testament reign of God. McDowell stresses this point: "It should be observed that the author [of the Revelation] thinks of Christ as possessing this lordship *now*. Certainly this assertion of the sovereignty of Jesus Christ cannot be referring to the future when he returns in his second advent. In the mind of the author he is king and sovereign *now*."[1]

3. What exactly is meant by the word "millennium"?

Since this study deals to such an extent with the millennium, we should take a closer look at the word itself, even though we've touched upon its definition in context a few times already. First of all, the word does not appear anywhere in the Bible. Its linguistic roots are in Latin and basically mean "a thousand years." (However, the Greek New Testament uses its word for a thousand, *chilia,* from which theologians have derived "chiliasm" and "chiliast," words we've already utilized in the present treatise.) This thousand-year restriction appears only in Revelation 20. Nevertheless, what is important in this passage regarding the "millennium" is not the length in years (which, again, is not supposed to be taken literally in a book so full of symbolic language), but

---

1. Edward A. McDowell, *The Meaning and Message of the Book of Revelation* (Nashville: Broadman Press, 1951, p. 26. All rights reserved. Used by permission.

rather the other characteristics: the reign of Christ with His saints midst of His enemies (Ps. 110:2; I Cor. 15:25) and the binding of Satan deceive the Gentiles no more. Hence, the amillennial view holds that the middle period of rule (the New Testament age) noted above is the millennium when Jesus governs His spiritual kingdom of believers for a very long time. We reign with Him (Rev. 20:4) because of His victory over Satan at the cross and because He has given us His authority over sin (I John 5:4-5). In other words, the church today is Christ's kingdom and the church age is identical with the millennium. The millennium is not a future physical kingdom under the rule of Jesus on earth in temporal Jerusalem, as the premillennialist contends.

Jay Adams sums it up for us: "Today he [Jesus] reigns and rules from the 'Jerusalem which is above' (Gal. 4:26); from that heavenly 'Mount Zion' to which the writer of Hebrews says that believers 'have come' (Heb. 12:22). There he sits as Zechariah's priest upon the throne (Zech. 6:12, 13); as David's greater Melchizedek (Ps. 110:1, 2, 3); as the King-Priest of Hebrews 8:1, who ministers not in an earthly millennial temple, but in the 'heavenly sanctuary, the true tabernacle which the Lord pitched, and not man' (Heb. 8:2)" *(The Time Is at Hand*, p. 27).

4. But what about all the presuppositions we've been taught? Like, isn't the millennium a thousand years long?

We alluded to this above. Considering that the Revelation (the only book in the Bible in which this number appears in reference to Christ's reign) is one of the most symbolic books in all of the Word of God, we should have little qualms about construing the actual number "1000" as figurative. Indeed, the number 1000 is used more than 20 times in Revelation, and not once is it meant literally. And even some of the "letteristic" premillennialists[2] take the locusts of chapter 9 metaphorically; they say that they're helicopters! In fact, others have understood verse 6 of the same chapter ("And they had hair like the hair of women. . . .") to mean that the locusts were "hippies"; this was a particularly popular opinion during the counter-cultural decade of the

---

2. Cf. Hal Lindsey's, *There's a New World Coming*.

"spiritualize" some passages in this highly imagistic
t spiritualizing a number? If the texts were obviously
d mood (as in a doctrinal section, for instance), then we
careful about interpreting them in a figurative sense; in
e difficult to do so and remain true to context at the same
time.   t of Revelation is so apocalyptic in nature, so bulging and
burgeoning with visions and symbols, that we shouldn't choose to
understand it literally unless the setting of its composition indicated as
much. (An example of the latter is the initial chapter, the first few verses,
where the writer speaks of himself and his immediate circumstances.)
William Barclay sees it this way, too: "We must not think that these
pictures are to be taken literally" (*The Revelation of John*, 2:18).

So, what we're saying is that the thousand years should not be construed as simply a series of centuries. We are not being modernistic or liberal here, because we're not rationalizing away any meaning. As we will show, all of what precedes Revelation 20 has been fulfilled. Therefore, we take the thousand-year reign of Jesus Christ to represent a very long period of time: it is the church age from our Lord's first advent until His second.

5. How about Satan? Wasn't he supposed to be bound during the millennium and, therefore, totally powerless?

Let's look at the main Bible verses to which premillennialists refer in this regard, in order to see exactly what they say: "And he [an angel] laid hold of the dragon, the serpent of old, who is the Devil and Satan, and bound him for a thousand years . . . so that he should not deceive the nations any longer" (Rev. 20:2-3). It is the last clause that is so often not included in the quote and which is precisely the clue to our interpretation: ". . . so that he should not deceive the nations any longer." (In the Bible, the word "nations" almost without exception indicates the Gentiles.)

Though explained before, this concept bears repeating: during the Old Testament era the Jews were the sole bearers of God's message of truth; the gentile world lay in the dark tight grip of Satan's lies. Then Jesus came! The Jews rejected His messiahship (His kingdom) because it didn't live up to their expectations, the result of faulty understanding of Old Testament prophecy. With that rejection, Israel relinquished her privileged role and ceased being the focal point of God's salvation. As Jesus Himself said, "The kingdom of God will be taken away from you [the Jews], and be given to a nation producing the fruit of it [the church]" (Matt. 21:43). The gentile world opened up to the divine truth, and ever since, God's kingdom has been spreading to all corners of the earth, and it has been a *gentile* church for the most part. Even the Old Testament prophets foresaw this change: "My name will be great among the nations" (Mal. 1:11), and, "Then it will come about in that day that the nations will resort to the root of Jesse [Jesus], Who will stand as a signal for the peoples" (Isa. 11:10). Our Lord made frequent reference to God's renunciation of Israel in His plan of the ages: "But the sons of the kingdom [the Jews] shall be cast out into outer darkness" (Matt. 8:12).

Thus was Satan bound (or restrained) in one way only, though it has proven to be a most efficacious restriction: he could no longer deceive the Gentiles as a whole in the same manner he could in the Old Testament era. The growth of the gospel into all nations proves this. We need only look at church history to note the colossal disparity between the spiritual condition of the Gentiles during the Old Testament and their involvement in the plan of God during the New Testament and thereafter. Of course, the Devil still has power to lie and to confuse, but more on an individual level and less on the national. Though some governments (e.g., the Soviet Union, Iran, Albania, India) explicitly oppose religious freedom (especially Christianity), the proportion is insignificant compared with the spiritual darkness in which the gentile world was immersed during the Old Testament era. And because of Jesus' victory over Satan at the cross, wherever the gospel charges, the devil must cower.

Also, the Bible uses very strong language to describe Jesus' present power over the devil. Colossians 2:15 asserts, "When He had disarmed the [spiritual] rulers and authorities, He made a public display of them, having triumphed over them through Him." And Hebrews 2:14 declares, "That through death He might render powerless him who had the power of death, that is, the devil" (see also John 12:31; Luke 10:18). This, in spite of I Peter 5:8, which states, "Your adversary, the devil, prowls about like a roaring lion, seeking someone to devour." Satan's activity continues, restless and malicious, but not without restraint, the sign of defeat already accomplished. Scripture itself says that the devil is in the world, but implies that he is vanquished: "Greater is He who is in you than he who is in the world" (I John 4:4). Grier agrees by referring to William Hendriksen, who alludes to "the Old Testament times when God suffered the nations to walk in their own ways (Acts 14:16) and . . . contrasts the widespread knowledge of Christ today."[3]

Perhaps a good summary of what we've been saying in response to this question comes from P. E. Hughes: "This [binding] is better understood, within the perspective of the New Testament, as referring to the present 'times of the Gentiles' when the Devil is held under restraint as the Gospel is preached to all nations" (*Interpreting Prophecy*, p. 110).

6. What about the tribulation?

Some amillennialists are of the futurist opinion that with the loosing of Satan a time of unequaled apostasy and antagonism toward the gospel will come before the end. But these are in the minority. Many believe that instead of a seven-year period of horror piled upon horror yet to come, the "great tribulation" spoken of in Matthew 24 (with parallel passages) and described in Revelation, as well as by some of the Old Testament prophets, has already happened. Once again, this latter view is likely entirely new (if not somewhat shocking) to you, but we hope to demonstrate in detail later how this may well be the case. Suffice it to say here that there has already occurred a period of years in history[4] when there was suffering as described in the Bible in apocalyptic language.

The Revelation was likely written about A.D. 65,[5] and it is probable that John was warning the Christians of his day that the Jews would be oppressing them for their faith and that the Romans were about to launch a crusade of annihilation against both the Jews and the church. He was also comforting his readers about God's ultimate protection against these

---

3. From W. J. Grier, *The Momentous Event* (Carlisle, Pa.: The Banner of Truth Trust, 1945), p. 114.
4. Nero's reign as Roman emperor, to be exact, A.D. 54 to 68, the last seven years of which were filled with cruel persecution toward the Christian community.
5. Some scholars claim a later date (90s), in which case the Tribulation could refer to the unparalleled persecution of the Christians under the Roman emperor Domitian.

antichrist forces. In fact, the writer of the last book in the Bible implies his own involvement in these circumstances: "I, John, your brother and fellow-partaker in the *tribulation* and *kingdom* . . ." (Rev. 1:9).

The preterist adherent to amillennialism considers the Revelation to be an extremely practical letter, albeit full of visionary language. However, even these figures of speech were for a reason: if such an Epistle could be understood by the enemy, it would never have reached the seven churches John wanted to inform. John puts the immediacy of his warning this way: "The time is near," found in 1:3 and reiterated in 22:10. The sufferings they were about to face, the "tribulation," was not two thousand years hence!

We spoke of the comprehensivist school of amillennial thought earlier, especially prevalent among the Protestant Reformers. It claims that the Apocalypse (the book of Revelation) is to be taken on a larger scale than a "practical letter," although the latter idea is not excluded. Mostly, comprehensivists believe that John's visions depict the forces of good and of evil at work throughout church history. Unlike the preterists, who perceive the Revelation chronologically, they are of the opinion that the millennium in chapter 20 encompasses the events of the preceding 16 chapters (4–19).

Ed Cox appears to be somewhat comprehensivist. He takes the tribulation in two ways: both the physical suffering of national Israel with the fall of Jerusalem and the spiritual suffering for the new Israel (Christendom) in the whole of the gospel age. He writes:

> This tribulation [for the church] has, in fact, already begun. It began with the first coming and will be terminated by the second advent of Christ. This is not to be confused with the great tribulation predicted by our Lord in Matthew 24:21. . . . These prophecies concerned national Israel and were fulfilled in 70 A.D. . . . Israel's [suffering] was physical; the church's is primarily spiritual" (*Biblical Studies in Final Things,* pp. 102-103).

Then he goes on to quote Ephesians 6:12, which reads, "For our struggle is not against flesh and blood, but against the rulers, against the powers, against the world-forces of this darkness, against the spiritual forces of wickedness in the heavenly places." This sounds like a reasonable position, especially in light of the loosing of Satan (Rev. 20:7-8), when there will be an intensification of this spiritual battle Christians now face daily.

There is yet a third amillennial view regarding the tribulation (and Antichrist) to which we referred initially. These adherents (e.g., W. J. Grier) believe that there will occur a specific time of unequaled physical persecution just prior to the end, though they too hold that the kingdom of Christ is not a corporeal dominion yet future, but rather a present spiritual reality represented in the church.

The Olivet Discourse (Matt. 24; Mark 13; Luke 21) describes the "great tribulation" in some detail, all of which the preterist perceives as explained by actual historical events. It is interesting that Jesus Himself uses the expression in reference to the fall of Jerusalem, which was to occur not 40 years later (Matt. 24:21 in direct context). Though entirely unfamiliar with Jesus' prophecies, the non-Christian Jewish historian Josephus was an unwitting commentator on the exact fulfillment of our Lord's predictions. He was an eyewitness to the destruction which befell the Holy City and recorded the holocaust faithfully. He wrote that the devastation was never equaled, not "from the beginning of the world" (*Wars of the Jews,* Bk. 5, chap. 10:5), thereby practically quoting Scripture (Matt. 24:21).

Most premillennialists understand the Olivet Discourse to be apocalyptic, that is, concerning the time just before the end (of the world, they say). This stems from the basic error of not interpreting Jesus' answers to the disciples' questions in light of the context of this discourse. At any rate, this view takes the sufferings Christ spoke of here as belonging to a future time of supernatural horror. Some of this passage may well be about the end of time, but not much of it;[6] most of it (at least) concerns the worst disaster any Jew could think of in Jesus' day: the ruin of their beloved city, Jerusalem, including the annihilation of the center of their religion, the temple.

We of the Western mind and with so much history behind us tend to underestimate the immensity of such a tragedy, and thus we don't identify the tribulation with the fall of the Holy City. But were we to study the record, we might see it the way Ellen White does: "Unhappy Jerusalem! rent by internal dissension, the blood of her children slain by one another's hands crimsoning her streets, while alien armies beat down her fortifications and slew her men of war! All the predictions given by Christ concerning the destruction of Jerusalem were fulfilled to the

---

6. Please see the more detailed discussion on Matt. 24, beginning page 65.

point concerning the beast's restoration to life is well taken, because Nero's death did not historically end his virulent influence, which lived on in the Roman Empire. It is significant that in Daniel 7:19ff., the word "beast" is in fact applied more generally to a kingdom (Rome).

Whatever the distinctions may be between these three titles (Antichrist, Son of Perdition, and the Beast), they are less important than their chronology, that is to say, how they fit into history: they represent figures and forces which fulfilled specific New Testament prophecies within the framework of ecclesiastical annals.

As noted earlier, the Holy Spirit through the writer of Revelation was warning people of that day about someone who would affect *them*, not their distant offspring. From the dating of the Apocalypse and the "number of the beast,"[8] we are of the opinion that the beast was an actual individual, Nero himself, one of the most diabolically evil men of all time. He slaughtered his own mother, his wife, and others of his own family, burned Christians alive, set Rome aflame (blaming the Christians!); the list of his atrocities is matched by very few in the history of mankind.

8. But we've always been taught that the millennium is to be a utopia. Isn't this true?

As illustrated above, traditional teaching isn't always founded upon God's Word. Likewise, this concept of the utopian nature of the millennium stems from faulty interpretation and presuppositions. Probably the main source of confusion stems from the binding-of-Satan teaching in Revelation 20:2. If he were totally out of the way, surely we'd experience a perfect type of existence, premillennialists argue (as if the devil were the only sin influence, ignoring biblical teaching that the "world" and the "flesh" hold their wicked sway, as well; James 4:4; Gal 5:17).

However, as pointed out earlier, if we remember in what unique way Satan was to be restrained during the millennium, light is shed on the

---

8. The number *666* (Rev. 13:18), an acrostic, or "word game," with a hidden message especially popular during apostolic times. ("Emperor Nero" works out to 666 in both Latin and Hebrew by taking letters as numbers.) As footnoted earlier, if a later date is set for the writing of Revelation, then Nero would be a "type" (for Domitian of the 90s).

meaning of this text: he is no longer permitted to deceive the Gentiles as a people. So the enemy isn't obliterated or out of the picture entirely, after all. He simply can't keep the Gentiles blind to the truth in the same manner he did in the Old Testament era. The gospel can now penetrate their dark hearts because of the cross.

T. Boersma agrees: "The imprisoned satan does enjoy a certain limited freedom of activity. He is limited in that he can 'deceive the nations no more' (Rev. 20:3). From the time of the ascension to the time of Christ's return, satan is not allowed to prevent the preaching of the gospel. Satan must retreat while the gospel advances across the globe" (*Is the Bible a Jigsaw Puzzle* . . . , p. 64).

A couple of Bible passages are warranted here to bring this point home. In Psalm 110:1-2 we read, "The Lord says to my Lord: 'Sit at My right hand, until I make Thine enemies a footstood for Thy feet. . . . Rule in the midst of Thine enemies.' " Look at that last clause: Jesus is told by the Father to rule *in the midst of His enemies!* If the millennium were supposed to be so utopian, there would be no enemy whatsoever. There would be no satanic influence. I Corinthians 15:25 corroborates this: "For He [Jesus] must reign *until* He has put all His enemies under His feet." And so today we see Jesus reigning over a kingdom or nation of priests (i.e., Christians; Rev. 1:6; I Pet 2:5) in the midst of a sinful world.

Furthermore, we are told in Revelation 20:7-8 that the devil would be loosed at the end to deceive the Gentiles once more. Many Christians these days declare that they see satanic power on the increase. (Of course, people have been saying this for centuries!) But if that were so, why has the enemy waited so long to augment his work? Surely he did not voluntarily restrain himself! The implication is that God is the one who has kept him in check in a manner unique to the church age and that He is perhaps beginning to release him even now. This is in line with the Reformed and amillennial view.

Dispensationalists are especially quick to point to the glowing descriptions in some of the Old Testament prophets which they assert refer to the glories of the messianic kingdom. They contend that they don't see these blessings today and, therefore, we are in fact not now experiencing the millennium. These texts which speak of a golden age are understood by the amillennialist in two ways: as depicting eternity in God's presence and/or spiritual blessings of the church. Jay Adams explains this, maintaining that the premillennialist

> confounds the millennium with the eternal state described in the last two chapters of Revelation, II Peter 3:12-13, Isaiah 65:17, and other prophecies. . . . The realized millennialist [amillennialist] does not think the millennial age is represented in Scripture as a golden period. He reads nothing about this in the one and only passage in which the one thousand years are mentioned. And from a study of the Apocalypse, he is convinced that the exposition of the twentieth chapter demands an identification of the thousand years with the so-called "Church age," and the golden age with the new heavens and the new earth of the last two chapters of that book (*The Time Is at Hand,* pp. 9-10).

Concerning Isaiah 11:4-9, O. T. Allis interprets the proverbial "lion and lamb" in terms of eternity: "Such a picture of an ideal age raises only one serious difficulty. It is whether the Bible and especially the New Testament predicts or allows for such a period of blessedness *before* the eternal state is ushered in, or whether the picture given to us by Isaiah is a description of the eternal state *itself* under earthly forms and images" (*Prophecy and the Church,* italics ours). Of course, Allis is of the latter opinion.

And as stressed over and over again in this treatise, some of the splendors about which the prophets wrote (Isa. 40; Zech. 14; Ezek. 38, etc.) have been fulfilled spiritually in the church, though they do not come all at once, but gradually—more like the slow process of a portrait than the instant but fleeting pictures on a TV tube.

Calvin is magnificent on this point. In his discussion on Jesus' prophecy about tribulations to come for the church (Matt. 24 and parallels), he writes,

> This might seem inconsistent with the entirely different descriptions of the Kingdom of Christ given by the prophets . . . (Is. 54:13, Joel 2:18, Jer. 31:34, Mal. 4:2). . . . We know that there are frequent passages where peace, justice, joy and abundance of all good things are promised. . . . So they were greatly deceived who wanted to have at the commencement of the Gospel an immediate and complete revelation of the things that we see being fulfilled from day to day (*Commentaries*).

Admittedly, in some cases it's difficult to distinguish between the two visionary directions (spiritual glories in the church and eternal blessedness in heaven), since the Old Testament prophets themselves appear at times to be perceiving both realms simultaneously, because the nature of the kingdom of Christ is but a shadow of the nature of heaven (I Cor. 13:12). And to make it even more complex, the prophets tend to use the same language to describe the wonders of these two domains. Let's not forget, too, that most of the promises God covenanted with national Israel were conditioned on her obedience and were therefore nullified by her faithlessness (Deut. 18:18-19; I Chron. 28:7-9; Ps. 89:30-32).

G. L. Murray writes that the dispensationalist "is following the Jewish method of interpretation which led its exponents to expect a literal fulfillment of every prophecy and which led them to reject and crucify their Messiah" (*Millennial Studies: A Search for Truth*, p. 40). We've already discussed the dangers of overliteralization. In reference to the millennium, it can lead us away from an understanding of the true nature of Christ's kingdom.[9]

Remember, we must interpret the Old Testament with the further enlightenment of the New. Who is true Israel, anyway? God's Word tells us that it is the Christian church. William Barclay stresses this point: "One of the basic thoughts of the New Testament is that the Church is the real Israel, and that the national Israel has lost all its privileges and promises to the Church" (*The Revelation of John*, 2:29). In Romans 2:28-29 we read, "For he is not a Jew who is one outwardly; neither is circumcision that which is outward in the flesh. But he is a Jew who is one inwardly; and circumcision is that which is of the heart, by the Spirit, not by the letter. . . ." And Romans 9:6 repeats the theme: "For they are not all Israel who are descended from Israel." Thus, the sacred oaths God gave to Israel which premillenarians have construed as blessings in a future millennium are in fact accomplished in us, children of Jacob by faith.

Not long before he died, Dr. G. Campbell Morgan came to this understanding. In a letter to the Rev. H. F. Wright, Morgan expressed this change of view: "I am convinced that all the promises made to Israel have found, are finding, and will find their perfect fulfillment in the Church. It is true that in the past, in my expositions, I gave a definite place to Israel in the purposes of God. I have now come to the conviction, as I have just said, that it is the new and spiritual Israel that is intended" (Archibald Hughes, *A New Heaven and a New Earth*, p. 123).

---

9. True Judaism in the Old Testament always extolled Jehovah, whereas Zionism extolls Israel as a nation. Dispensationalism tends toward Zionism.

But some of us have forgotten this teaching. We've clung to the erroneous vision of a physical, national, and utopian Israel on earth some day hence. We've made the same mistake the Jews did upon rejecting Jesus' spiritual kingship. They missed their Messiah, though he was right before their eyes! We're missing our King, though He *is* king indeed! And by denying His present-day kingdom, we deny that He came as Messiah, for they are one and the same: the messianic kingdom and the millennium. After all, only *one* kingdom was prophesied in the Old Testament (Dan. 2:44).

One of the Jewish characters in the marvelous musical, *Fiddler on the Roof*, made the pathetic remark that if ever God were to send His Messiah, the time to do so would have been then, when the little Russian town of Jews was under Czarist persecution. Upon hearing those words, the present writers fairly cried out in response, "He already has come!" But when Christians pray for Jesus to come to reign in His kingdom, we would cry out as well, "He already is King!"

9. Aren't there supposed to be signs announcing the coming of the millennial kingdom?

Believe it or not, the Bible doesn't mention *any* signs, at least not of the variety popularly conceived. As a matter of fact, Jesus taught quite the opposite. Luke 17:20-21 reads, "Now having been questioned by the Pharisees as to when the kingdom of God was coming, He answered them and said, 'The kingdom of God is not coming with signs to be observed; nor will they say, "Look, here it is!" or, "There it is!" For behold, the kingdom of God is in your midst.' " There we have it, from incarnate Deity! Not only is the kingdom of God not to be established with visible signs, but our Lord implies that people won't even recognize its presence in spite of the fact that it is already in their midst. The kingdom of God under Jesus Christ was not established by warfare or political uprising, nor under the aegis of any earthly government. Rather, it was introduced so subtly that just about everyone missed it, and yet it wasn't so subtle to those who recognized it. It was a mighty spiritual event that ultimately turned the world upside-down; it is as profound as the new birth. Let's make sure *we* don't fail to acknowledge this kingdom, too.

Needless to say, this doesn't mean that signs weren't given at all about anything. Oh how Jesus' contemporaries loved to see signs and wonders (John 4:48)! And our Lord often obliged them. One metaphor He chose to use was that of the fig tree, sometimes symbolic of the Israelite nation. For instance, perhaps by cursing the unfruitful fig tree (Matt 21:19), Jesus was saying Israel would likewise be judged for her fruitlessness. (This could apply to individuals just as well.) And it is possible that the parable of the barren fig tree in Luke 13:6-9 means the same thing. However, merely because the fig tree might refer to Israel once in a while, it does not automatically follow that every time a fig tree is mentioned, Israel is intended. In point of fact, the fig-tree image of Israel has been greatly overstated. For example, in the Olivet Discourse Jesus refers to the blooming of the fig tree as a sign of summer. Contrary to popular belief, this has nothing to do with the "blossoming" (reestablishment) of the nation Israel prior to the second advent. We know this from the text itself; Luke 21:29 tells us that Jesus added, "And *all* these trees." Had He meant Israel, He would not have generalized the statement, especially if the fig tree always concerned that nation. As a matter of fact, neither the fig tree nor Israel is even the subject of Christ's prophecy, but simply an illustration for the discussion (concerning the fall of Jerusalem) that immediately precedes it.

It's interesting to note that the well-worn phrase, "the signs of the times," appears only once in the Bible (Matt. 16:3), and it has more to do with what had already happened back then and with what was at that time happening than with what would yet happen. In this verse, Jesus was actually rebuking the Pharisees and Sadducees for being woefully ignorant about Him because they willfully misunderstood the "signs" or the prophecies. Hoekema comments, "On the basis of these 'signs of the times,' the Jewish leaders should have realized that the great, decisive event in history had occurred with the coming of the Messiah" (*The Bible and the Future,* p. 128). Yes, signs were given, but more often than not, they concerned our Lord's first advent, His "visitation" as God in our midst.

Some of these signs—that is to say, the proofs that Christ's kingdom has come to earth—are suggested by Hoekema: "One such sign is *the casting out of demons* by Jesus. . . . Another sign is the *fall of Satan*. . . . Still another sign of the presence of the kingdom was *the performance miracles* by Jesus and his disciples. . . . Another sign, even more important than the last, was *the preaching of the gospel.* . . . *The bestowal of the forgiveness of sins* is a sign of the presence of the kingdom . . ." *(The Bible and the Future,* pp. 46-47). In Matthew 11 and Luke 7, John the Baptist's disciples came to Jesus inquiring as to whether He really was the "expected One." Instead of a direct response, Jesus maintained that He was even then fulfilling messianic prophecies (Isa. 29:18; 35:5; 61:1) by giving the blind their sight and by preaching the gospel to the poor. So Jesus did far more than answer with a yes; He *demonstrated* that His kingdom had in fact arrived. His works were the signs of the kingdom of God. Indeed, Jesus Himself was the sign—the only necessary sign—of the messianic kingdom!

10. What about all the signs in Matthew 24?

The amillennial view is not without its difficulties, although there are relatively few compared to the confusing maze set up by the premillennialist. The twenty-fourth chapter of Matthew is one of the more complicated passages of the Bible, but it was likely far more comprehensible to our Lord's contemporaries than it is to the Western mind, especially of today. In fact, this disparity between the ancient Eastern mentality and ours is one of the main causes for so much misunderstanding of this Olivet Discourse. For instance, the word "coming" in verse 3 probably meant something other than the second advent to the disciples, since the latter weren't even told (except by inference in parables) about the parousia until the ascension in Acts 1. Note that the parallel question in Mark 13 and Luke 21 is phrased differently—without the word "coming" and implying judgment. Boersma writes:

> When the Bible speaks about a "coming" of the Lord Jesus, we immediately think of His return. But here Christ spoke to the disciples about the coming of the Son of man in a more immediate context. Matthew 10:23 helps to make this clear: "When they persecute you in one town, flee to the next; for truly, I say to you, you will not have gone through all the towns of Israel, before the Son of man comes." In other words, Christ says that the Son of man will "come" even before the disciples will have traveled in missionary capacity to all of the towns of Israel *(Is the Bible a Jigsaw Puzzle* . . . , p. 80).

Furthermore, it is reasonable to consider that the apocalyptic language Jesus uses in verses 29-31 regarding cosmic events was understood by the Eastern mind as underscoring the great significance of His prophecy. Therefore, unless interpreted in light of symbolic speech, these predictions could appear as exaggerations if they don't come to pass exactly as stated. Of course, this is impossible, since Jesus cannot lie. God rarely—if ever—has accomplished His purposes the way mankind has popularly thought, and so we would do well to learn a lesson: accept figurative language as intended, concrete pictures of abstractions. Only then can we begin to analyze a passage such as this one.

For instance, Jesus quotes words (Matt. 24:29) depicting astronomical holocaust and celestial cataclysm out of Isaiah and Ezekiel. Let's look closer at these Old Testament texts. Ezekiel 32:7 speaks of stars and the sun and the moon in catastrophic terms with reference to a prediction for the ruin of Egypt by the Medes. This prophecy came to pass about 570 B.C., but such cosmic miracles didn't actually take place. The same can be said for Isaiah's warning (chap. 13) that Babylon would fall; this occurred about 535 B.C., 200 years yet future to his cry. The apocalyptic language in verse 10 is part of that prophecy, which was fulfilled to the letter, but once again, the sun and the moon and the stars were not altered that day. Adam Clarke explains, "The Hebrew poets, to express happiness, prosperity, the advancement of states, kingdoms, and potentates, make use of images taken from the most striking parts of nature, from the heavenly bodies, from the sun, moon, and stars. . . . On the contrary, the destruction of kingdoms is represented by opposite images. The stars are obscured, the moon withdraws her light, and the sun shines no more! The earth quakes, and the heavens tremble; and all things seem tending to their original chaos" (*Clarke's Commentary*).

Furthermore, Peter quotes apocalyptic descriptions out of Joel (chap. 2) in the second chapter of Acts and claims their fulfillment in Pentecost. We all know there is no report of the moon's turning to blood, nor of the sun's becoming dark that day. So what could Peter mean by asserting that Joel's words were accomplished even then? You see, because he was an ancient Jew, he didn't think the way we do. He had no problem with this "exaggeration"; he certainly wasn't lying under the inspiration of the Holy Spirit. What he was doing was emphasizing the "cosmic" nature of the spiritual event that was taking place: the outpouring of God's Spirit on "all flesh." Please note that this is not *our* interpretation, but rather Peter's: apostolic, inspired, infallible.

With all of this in mind by way of introduction, let's be careful not to mold the rest of Scripture to conform to involved texts like Matthew 24. Instead, the serious student of the Word should interpret these difficult passages in view of the clearer teachings elsewhere in Scripture. An excellent example is a comparison between the somewhat intricate prophecies Jesus makes in the Olivet Discourse with His statement in Luke 17, discussed above. In the former, He gives all kinds of signs about events yet future *to Him,* but in the latter He refutes signs for the kingdom of God altogether, as we have seen. We must infer, therefore, that this text before us *directly* concerns itself with things *other than* the establishment of His messianic kingdom. With this basic premise, we will touch upon a few more ideas in regard to the topic at hand.

Three questions were posed to our Lord in the Matthew passage, whereas only two appear in the Mark and Luke parallels. Therefore, we should interpret Matthew 24 in conjunction with Mark 13 and Luke 21. By so doing, we eliminate any Jewish "two-age" influences that might have played a part in Matthew's account, since the latter apostle was writing mainly to Hebrew Christians.

The three queries (in Matthew) could be paraphrased as follows: "When will these things be?" (the destruction of the temple), "What will be the sign of Your coming?" (likely a "judgment coming," e.g., the fall of Jerusalem), and "What will be the sign of the end of the age?" (some perceive this as the second coming, while others take it to mean the end of the *Jewish* era, which would then put this answer in the same time period as the first two replies).

Now, let's take a look at the parallel questions in Mark and Luke. The first is the same: "When will these things be?" This was asked directly in response to Jesus' statement that the temple would be torn down. Thus, the context of this query (with its answer) refers to that event, the fall of Jerusalem. The second question, however, seems to be nothing like either of the next two in the Matthew text. Mark and Luke put it something like this: "What will be the sign when this will be fulfilled (or come to pass)?" This phraseology is far more comprehensible than Matthew's, considering what Jesus had just been saying. It is most natural that the disciples would want to know all they could about our Lord's implication that the temple would be destroyed. Matthew's questions *appear* less appropriate to the context, because of the words "coming" and "end of the age." We tend to interpret these latter terms in accordance with popular theology of our day: "coming" means Jesus' second advent, and "end of the age" means the end of the world. But in view of the fact that these two Matthew questions are parallel to Mark's and Luke's second question (which do not incorporate any hint of a "coming" or of "the end of the age"), we should look for alternate interpretations to Matthew's terminology. After all, language isn't mathematics; a word or phrase can have more than one meaning. We've already noted that "coming" probably means that Jesus would *come* to judge Israel's incredulity. The "end of the age" is likely limited to the end of the *Jewish* age (i.e., the Gentiles become the "elect" or "chosen people," the physical sign of which would be the total devastation of the Holy City). So, this judgment on the Jews (that their unique relationship to God was about to end) was a direct result of their unbelief and is in line with Christ's prophecy.

Nevertheless, most Bible commentators seem to agree that Jesus may be dealing with two time periods here, both of them judgments: one to take place in A.D. 70 (which makes reply to the first two of Matthew's queries) and the other at His final return or when time will cease to be (the answer to the last of the three questions). However, most events at least were fulfilled within a 40-year period: many false Christs did come in His name, the disciples were in fact delivered up to persecution (some recorded in the Acts), Judeans did indeed flee the city for the mountains, Jerusalem was surrounded by armies, the temple was utterly destroyed, and so forth.

Hoekema, an amillennial scholar, believes that the Olivet Discourse "exemplifies the principles of prophetic foreshortening. . . . The signs mentioned in them will have a further fulfillment at the time of the Parousia. In the meantime, all the signs of the times described in the New Testament characterize the entire period between Christ's first and second coming" (*The Bible and the Future*, p. 131). As you can see, his view is somewhat comprehensivist.

On the other hand, dispensationalists take most, if not all, of Matthew 24 futuristically. This is to say that all of Jesus' prophecies have yet to be accomplished in the tribulation which is to precede a physical millennium. They claim verses like Matthew 24:30, where the Son of man will be seen "coming on the clouds of the sky," as referring to the second advent. Now this may be the case, but the Greek verb here for "come" encompasses the idea of moving: to go or to come. It is not one of the three words the New Testament employs for the second coming. With reference to Daniel 7:13-14, where the Son of man is seen ascending to the Ancient of Days (the Father) to receive a kingdom, we understand this verse to speak of Jesus' ascension (Acts 1:9), not His return. Such an interpretation would put this verse (30) into the historic framework of Christ's first advent, as well.

At any rate, by ignoring the time context of our Lord's replies, the futurist demands *duplication* of historic circumstances and events in order to create again the proper conditions for fulfillment: restoration of the Roman Empire, rebuilding of the temple, reinstitution of Mosaic sacrifices, etc. Hence, Hal Lindsey (as well as others of his opinion) "is able to read a lot of things into the text that are simply not there" (T. Boersma, *Is the Bible a Jigsaw Puzzle* . . . , p. 77).

The disciples obviously didn't understand what Jesus was talking about here, either, not until after Pentecost. Once again, it is because of the Eastern mentality that they automatically linked the destruction of Jerusalem to an immediate realization of apocalyptic bliss. Calvin felt that it was understandable for the disciples to tie the two prophecies so closely at this point in their spiritual comprehension, since at the mere mention of the demise of their beloved city, surely the new age of Israel's glory would be ushered in. (And indeed a new age was ushered in, but not the way they thought!) Calvin writes regarding the Olivet Discourse:

> He [Jesus] was left with the task of raising another far more splendid temple, a far more prosperous state of the Kingdom, as had been foretold by the prophets. . . . It was more than the disciples could believe that the magnificent splendour of the present temple would give place to Christ. . . . We must note, since they had considered from childhood that the temple would stand to the end of time and had the idea deeply rooted in their minds, that they had not thought that the temple could fall down as long as the world's created order stood (*Commentaries*).

But by prophesying destruction for Jerusalem, Jesus was making it clear once for all that any thought of a future physical kingdom in that city had to be quashed. His kingdom was to be spiritual, and to make sure that it be understood that way, the city from which the Jews expected a glorious state to spring would shortly fall to ruin.

Adam Clarke took the extreme preterist view that absolutely all of this discourse was fulfilled before A.D. 100. In other words, the pestilences and famines and earthquakes (v. 7) accompanied the end of the Jewish age, that is, A.D. 70. There does appear to be historical evidence for this (e.g., the volcano Vesuvius erupted over Pompeii in A.D. 79). Josephus records countless Zealot insurrections followed by Roman attacks on rebellious Israelite cities. Clarke includes the more "cosmic" signs of verses 29-31 in this view as well, by perceiving them figuratively, whereas Josephus alludes to visible phenomena that could corroborate a more literal interpetation: "Before sun-setting, chariots and troops of soldiers in their armour were seen running about among the clouds, and surrounding of cities" (*Wars of the Jews,* Bk. 6, chap. 5:3). He goes on to mention "quaking" and a supernatural "sound as of a great multitude." So, considering the fact that Jesus stated, "This generation will not pass away until *all* these things take place" (Matt. 24:34), Clarke's position seems reasonable.

Thus we see that there are varying opinions among amillennialists regarding just how far Jesus' predictions here were fulfilled in early times, but all concur that *most* of the Olivet Discourse is to be understood in the framework of first-century history. Therefore, though many signs were given by the Lord Jesus Christ in this prophetic discourse, they do *not* concern a future physical millennium.

11. What about the last days? Don't they have signs?

We hear so much about the "last days" anymore, but it has become a sadly misunderstood, catch-all phrase. Before we go any further, let's see what the Bible means by it.

Originally, it was an Old Testament term which very often referred to the messianic reign. A prophet of the old covenant saw only two eras in God's economy: *his* "now," and *his* "last days," or sometime in the future from his perspective. And *his* "last days" have become *our* "now," because upon close scrutiny none of these Old Testament passages has to do with the end of all time. Later, the New Testament disciples picked up this Old Testament expression and used it in their own writings.

As we have seen, the apostle Peter interprets Joel's prophecy (Joel

2:28-32) as denoting the last days, and he attributes those last days to his contemporary situation. Peter says in Acts 2:16 that Joel's sign for the "last days" (the outpouring of the Holy Spirit on all flesh) was happening right then and there. You see, such a blessing of the Holy Spirit in abundance was not part of the Old Testament experience, not to the everyday lay person at least, so this was a stupendous event Joel saw prophetically. We tend to take this tremendous blessing for granted today, we who are the very temple of the Holy Spirit. We're so used to this marvelous condition, you might say, so spoiled, that we have no real comprehension of what it must have been like without the *Paraclete* (Greek for "Comforter," a New Testament term for the Holy Spirit). Hence, with this utterance, Joel was describing something yet future to him and entirely new. How thrilling it must have been for him to foresee this! And what an honor it must have been for Peter to have been among the first to experience it, to preach it, to die for it!

At any rate, by applying Joel's words to Pentecost, Peter was claiming to be witness to their fulfillment. Therefore, the popular but misunderstood phrase, "last days," does not here mean the time right at the end, full of signs such as wars and rumors of wars, pestilences, famines, earthquakes, etc. In fact, we've just seen that the scriptural context where these signs appear (Olivet Discourse) has to do with none other than the fall of Jerusalem. Besides, have not holocausts and calamities been with us down through the ages? The Crusades, the Black Plague, the Inquisition, Vesuvius, the Thirty Years' War, Hitler's Jewish extermination, to name but a few! These are just the earth groaning with sin (Rom. 8:22), so such events should not be perceived eschatologically. In point of fact, the last days began in apostolic times and have continued on down through the New Testament age, God's kingdom under the reign of the Son. O. T. Allis agrees: "Joel's words do concern the Church, . . . (*Prophecy and the Church*, p. 136).

It is significant that "last days" is sometimes translated "latter days," or "days to come" in the Old Testament, depending on the version. Since the same Greek term (*eschatos*, LXX[10]) is used in all cases, we are persuaded that the English phrases themselves are basically interchangeable, though the exact time allusion may differ.

---

10. LXX stands for the Septuagint, the Greek translation of the Old Testament Scriptures, 250–100 B.C.

(Cf. Gen. 49:1; Num. 24:14; Jer. 23:20; Ezek. 38:16; Mic. 4:1.) It is important to remember that "in none of the passages does the expression . . . refer directly to the final period of world history" (Boersma, *Is the Bible a Jigsaw Puzzle* . . . , p. 43). Most of these Old Testament texts speak of the Messiah's visitation and the establishment of His spiritual kingdom (the church) immediately subsequent to it, while others vary in meaning, all of which belong to either ancient or contemporary history from our viewpoint.

In addition, "last days" (plural) should be distinguished from "last day" (singular), whenever the latter applies to the end. (By the way, "last day" shows up only in the Gospel of John.) As shown, the last days have already begun, whereas the last day refers to an event yet future: the second coming, including both the rapture[11] and the final judgment. In John 6:39, 40, 44, and 54, Jesus speaks of the resurrection of the righteous in the "last day." (See also John 11:24; 12:48.)

Other expressions used in the New Testament are "last time(s)" and "last hour," both of which usually mean this present age[12] (John 7:37; I Pet. 1:20; I John 2:18). We offer all of this information to illustrate one point: we must not be inflexible about all this terminology. In English we may use a variety of words to mean one thing, and we may use one word to mean a variety of things. And so it is in any language, including Greek and Hebrew, the two original tongues of the Bible.

Getting back to the original term, Acts 2 is not the only New Testament text that tells us we're in the last days. Hebrews 1:2 is unmistakable: "[God] *in these last days* has spoken to us in His Son." (See also James 5:3 and II Pet. 3:3.) Though the phrase "last days" doesn't appear in Hebrews 9:26, its implication is even stronger: "He [Jesus] has appeared once for all *at the end of the age* to put away sin by the sacrifice of himself" (Revised Standard Version). This says that there is no future epoch whatsoever left for us in world history. In other words, this gospel age is the final stage in God's plan for earth. Any scriptural reference to "this age" and to "the age to come" encompasses the idea of the present church era and of eternity, hence only three ages (Old Testament, New

---

11. The root meaning of "rapture" is "carry away." In Christian circles, it has come to be identified with Christ's second coming, when our Lord receives us: "The dead in Christ shall rise first. Then we who are alive and remain shall be *caught up* together with them in the clouds to meet the Lord in the air" (I Thess. 4:16-17).

12. With one exception, I Pet. 1:5, referring to the future.

Testament, eternity) not four—or more—as premillennialists would insist (Old Testament, New Testament, the millennium, eternity). (See Mark 10:30; Luke 20:34-36; I Cor. 10:11; Eph. 1:21; Heb. 2:5.)

12. How do Daniel's 70 weeks of years fit into eschatology?

This complex prophecy appears in Daniel 9. It is not nearly as difficult to understand as it might seem at first, though, especially if the passage is read *naturally* (taking historical, cultural, and linguistic elements into consideration). We've alluded to the importance of context already, and it cannot be stressed too much. For instance, if someone were to find an old letter in a book he'd picked up at a second-hand store, its contents would have little meaning to him unless he knew the circumstances of its writing: Who wrote to whom? When was it written? What were the events surrounding the subject? and so forth. In other words, the context would be invaluable for its "interpretation." In the same way this is true of all Scripture, especially a text such as this. So let's take a look at the circumstances which shaped this chapter.

Daniel was taken captive into Babylon in the year 606 B.C. Over 60 years later (chap. 9), he is reading Jeremiah's remarkable prophecy (Jer. 25:11-12), promising that Israel's captivity would last only 70 years. In response to Daniel's earnest prayer that follows (imploring God to honor Jeremiah's words), the angel Gabriel informs him that a timetable has been set, one that reaches beyond Israel's *physical* captivity into her *spiritual* captivity, that is to say, her faithlessness. He says (v. 24) that God has determined 70 weeks (of years)[13] for Messiah's advent onto Israelite soil. The starting point for this exact length of time is the issuance of a decree to rebuild Jerusalem. It is a historical fact that Artaxerxes (a Persian king whose empire had by now conquered Babylon) made such a decree in 457 B.C. (Ezra 7:11).

Gabriel divides these 70 heptads (weeks of years) into three unequal parts. The first is seven "weeks" (49 years), the period of time it took Ezra and Nehemiah to see to the completion of Jerusalem's restoration

---

13. This is called a "heptad," signifying a unit of seven; Lev. 25:8 tells us Israel had "sabbatic" years, by which Jewish years were combined into groups of seven. Therefore, 70 weeks of years amount to 70 times 7, or 490 years.

and reformation (408 B.C.). The second division of time is 62 "weeks" (434 years), which takes us right up to A.D. 26. After correcting for the Dionysian calendar error of four years, we arrive at the year 30, when Messiah Jesus began His public ministry (Luke 3:23). The third and final set of "weeks" is the shortest: only one heptad, in the middle of which "Messiah will be cut off and have nothing" (v. 26). In other words, 33½ is the age at which Jesus was to die. The accuracy of this prophecy is startling.

Now we go on to see what else the angel says. He informs Daniel that the Messiah would "make a firm covenant with the many" (v. 27); we take this to be Jesus' ministry of salvation to those who would hear. In the middle of this seventieth "week," Messiah's death would "put a stop to sacrifice" (v. 27); by this we understand that Jesus' crucifixion would put an end once and for all to Mosaic sacrifices (Heb. 7:27). Any oblations[14] that followed His death would not only be inefficacious, but abominable, in that they betray a rejection of the ultimate sacrifice.

Furthermore, this prophecy speaks of what the messianic ministry would constitute. Verse 24 tells us He would "finish the transgression," "make an end of sin," and "make atonement for iniquity." It is clear the cross is pictured here. The writer of Hebrews likely had this very prophecy in mind when he wrote of Jesus: "Now once at the consummation of the ages He has been manifested to put away sin by the sacrifice of Himself" (Heb. 9:26). Young asserts, "These three words [transgression, sin, iniquity] well represent in its fulness the nature of that curse which has separated man from God. The first stated purpose of the decreeing of the period of 70 sevens is to abolish this curse. . . . How is this to be accomplished? The text does not say, but who, in the light of the NT revelation, can read these words without coming face to face with that one perfect sacrifice . . . ?" (*The Prophecy of Daniel*, p. 199).

And continuing on further in verse 24, we read that the Messiah would "bring in everlasting righteousness" (a picture of the victory of the cross), He would "seal up vision and prophecy" (fulfilling every messianic promise), and He would "anoint the most holy place" (possibly a reference either to Christ's making each Christian's heart into a pure temple for communion with God—Heb. 9:14, or to His entering the true

---

14. Other than spiritual; cf. Ps. 51:16-17 and Rom. 12:1.

tabernacle, which is in heaven, with His own blood—Heb. 9:11, 12). Regarding this "anointing," Adam Clarke offers another interesting interpretation: "Here it means the consecration . . . of our blessed Lord, the Holy One of Israel, to be the Prophet, Priest, and King of mankind" (*Clarke's Commentary*).

Gabriel even goes on to predict the fall of Jerusalem directly consequent to Israel's "cutting off" of the Messiah, that is to say, His crucifixion. Verse 26 informs us that "the people of the prince who is to come will destroy the city and the sanctuary." Historically, that "prince" was Titus, the Roman general cited earlier, who besieged Jerusalem in A.D. 70, and his "people" were the Romans.[15]

Thus we see here a prophetic overview of the ancient history of Israel. There really is not much of a problem in comprehending these verses when studied within the framework of history, culture, and language. However, a very different interpretation has evolved from the dispensational school of thought, which agrees that this prophecy came to pass as we've just explained, but only up until the middle of the seventieth "week." Exponents of such a view see difficulty in clauses like "make an end of sin" and "bring in everlasting righteousness." Once again, they overliteralize, and (failing to perceive the spiritual application in the faithful elect of God, true Israel) they visualize rather a sinless utopia, which is automatically equated with a future millennium. Therefore, they artificially suspend the completion of the seventieth heptad until thousands of years later at the end of the world. This is where the term "great parenthesis" comes in, because between the four-hundred-eighty-sixth (and a half) year of Gabriel's prediction (33½ years after Christ's birth) and the end, a parenthetical temporal unit of unspecified length (almost 2000 years, so far) must be inserted to keep their chronology intact.

Moreover, Young establishes that, regarding the six messianic roles enumerated in verse 24, "the very purpose of decreeing the sevens is to finish the transgression, etc., and . . . these things are to be accomplished *before* the expiry of the 70 sevens, although the blessings brought about thereby may continue for long after that expiry. . . . The six items presented in this verse are all Messianic. . . . The termination of

---

15. And the following verse (27) goes on to predict the ultimate fall of Rome herself: "On the wings of abominations will come one who makes desolate, even until a complete destruction . . . is poured out on the one who makes desolate."

the 70 sevens coincides then, not . . . with the end of the present age, the 2nd Advent of our Lord, but with His 1st Advent" (*The Prophecy of Daniel,* pp. 197, 201, italics ours).

And once again we face the tremendous disparity between the modern Occidental mind and the ancient Oriental way of thinking. If we take into account that the angel was dividing prophecy into *heptads* (weeks of years) and *not* into years (which are easier for us to understand because they are the normal temporal units we use), the prediction is accomplished *in its entirety* right through the seventieth "week," since it was in the middle of that "week" that the Messiah was "cut off"; so instead of a three-and-a-half-year chunk of time left dangling, there is no more *full* heptad to be considered.

One might ask why the numbers in a passage out of such a symbolic book as Daniel should be taken so exactly "at face value." We would answer that first of all, unlike chapters 2, 7, and 10ff., Daniel 9 is not a dream or a vision. Gabriel is presenting a clear outline of the future, a straight prediction; in fact, it is a verbatim quote with no human intermediary. Besides, Daniel had just been reading a literal prediction out of Jeremiah when the angel appeared to him. This sets the stage for the ensuing prophecy, the one we've just been studying.

13. What does the "Abomination of Desolation" mean?

Like the terms "tribulation" and "antichrist," the "abomination of desolation" has come to have an extremely narrow meaning among premillennialists, who claim it refers to an apocalyptic event: the establishment of antichrist-worship in the temple of God. They believe this will occur during the great tribulation to come and that it represents a profanation of the holy places in Jerusalem's temple. Whereas we agree that this phrase does incorporate the concept of defiling the holy, we would not place it into the scheme of futurist eschatology.

Although the actual phrase "abomination of desolation" appears only a few times in the Bible (Dan. 11:31; 12:11; Matt. 24:15; Mark 13:14), the term is implied in other contexts as well (Ezek. 33:29; Dan. 9:27, etc.). It is important to realize, though, that such an abomination has already been fulfilled—both historically and spiritually. For instance, in

586 B.C. Nebuchadnezzar's Babylonian forces invaded the Jewish temple and carried off the sacred vessels (II Chron. 36:7; cf. Dan. 5:23); the Holy City was sacked by fire at this time. Then in 169 B.C. Antiochus Epiphanes the Greek entered the holy place and sacrificed a pig (anathema to the Jew) on the altar (I Macc. 1:20-24). We have already taken a look at the fall of Jerusalem in A.D. 70, when Titus brought the temple to utter ruin (Josephus, *Wars of the Jews,* Bk. 6). In each of these historic cases, a *desolation* (destruction) took place, during which there was an *abomination* (defilement of the holy). Hence, the phrase "abomination of desolation."

But what was Jesus really talking about in the Olivet Discourse (Matt. 24; Mark 13; Luke 21) when He spoke of the "abomination of desolation"? Surely He had far more in mind than the actual presence of Titus and his Roman legions standing in the holy places. And we are convinced He wasn't denoting an event that wouldn't even happen until thousands of years had passed. As we have seen, the context forbids such an interpretation since it deals directly with the fall of Jerusalem. Wouldn't Jesus be referring to the continuation of Mosaic sacrifice beyond His own death on the cross? Whether it is Satan who the prophet says has always wanted to "sit on the mount of assembly" (Isa. 14:13) and be "like the Most High" (Isa. 14:14), or simply Nebuchadnezzar, we can't be sure, but we do know that the devil has never stopped coveting God's throne. Hence, any temple oblation performed subsequent to the crucifixion would in a sense be dedicated to Satan.

In regards to the term *abomination,* Young writes, "The word must be used figuratively to describe the worship of the Temple after the veil had been rent in twain. No longer was this the house of the Lord, but a house of abominations, for the true worship of Jehovah had ceased" (*The Prophecy of Daniel,* p. 218).

So, God rent the veil of the temple in two, signifying thereby that the Holy of Holies (*kodesh kodashim* in Hebrew, the innermost temple sanctuary, where God "dwelt," I Kings 8:13) was profaned by Israel's unbelief. But it was more than that. God was saying the temple wasn't holy any more *because His Son* had just become the *Sacrifice to end all sacrifices.* The torn veil was a sign both of God's wrath toward Israel's faithlessness and of His approval of Jesus' death, opening the real sanctuary ("true tabernacle," Heb. 8:2) to all who would believe. It was Jehovah's way of showing mankind that the Holiest One of all that is holy was made to be sin (II Cor. 5:21). God in hell, this is surely the greatest of all abominations of desolation!

14. What is the book of Revelation all about?

Admittedly this answer will be somewhat scanty according to the limitations set for our study, but that needs be the case for the sake of brevity. This Epistle is generally thought to have been written sometime in the 90s under the reign of Domitian, but many hold that it was recorded before the destruction of the Holy City, since the temple was apparently still standing (Rev. 11:1), being measured for ruin, a procedure not uncommon in Bible times (e.g., II Sam. 8:2). Also, verse 2 says that the city was *yet to be* trodden down by the Gentiles for 42 months, or 3½ years. (The wording here is nearly identical to Jesus' prediction of the destruction of the Holy City in the Olivet Discourse; Luke 21:24). A further indication of the earlier dating is the acrostic "666," previously footnoted as the "number of the beast" of Revelation 13:18, which is the sum of Nero's name and title in Hebrew and Latin. Nero was in fact the Roman emperor during the 50s and 60s.

The Revelation has sustained some of the severest misunderstanding of all books in the Bible. This is so because it is read out of context and is forced into a preconceived and incorrect system of eschatology. For the most part, premillennialists ignore the outline our risen Lord gave to John right at the outset,[16] and they insist that the whole of the message from chapter 4 through the last remains a prophecy yet to be fulfilled at the end of time. The fact remains, though, that most of the Revelation deals with either the time contemporary to John's day (chaps. 2, 3), or immediately subsequent to it[17] (chaps. 4–19). Only the final two chapters (21, 22) embrace the end of all time, swinging out into eternity, while chapter 20 spans the church age.

The books of Daniel and of Revelation are closely associated in many

---

16. Rev. 1:19 says, "Write therefore the things which you *have* seen, and the things which *are*, and the things which *shall* take place after these things."

17. Rev. 1:1 tells us, "The Revelation of Jesus Christ, which God gave Him to show to His bondservants, the things which must *shortly* take place."

ways, but the Old Testament prophecy was *sealed* up precisely because its predictions were *not* to be fulfilled right away (Dan. 12:4, 9), whereas the Revelation was *unsealed* because the time of accomplishment was imminent.[18] Also, they are both apocalyptic books, first because their language is highly figurative and visionary, and second because they deal with the end of an age. Many misconstrue this latter characteristic, insisting that all apocalypses deal with the end of the world altogether. But in fact, Daniel has nothing to do *at all* with the termination of this physical earth, just with the end of the *Jewish* age (followed by the inception of the gospel age), the outward sign of which was the fall of Jerusalem. Likewise, as we will be demonstrating, John's Revelation has little to do with the end of all time, concentrating for the most part on the same issue, that is, the close of the Jewish era, which was contemporary to the writer's day.

The prophet Daniel records four world empires that would follow chronologically one upon the other (chaps. 2, 7, 10ff.): Babylon, Medo-Persia, Greece, and Rome. He tells us that "in the days of those kings [referring to the fourth kingdom, Rome] the God of heaven will set up a kingdom which will never be destroyed" (Dan. 2:44). Therefore, during the rule of that fourth empire,[19] Jesus, God incarnate, would come to earth to introduce a new covenant (the "new testament") whereby mankind could live righteously by faith. It was during the Roman years that Christ established His kingdom. And this is exactly where Revelation picks up its story. What was far off for Daniel was near at hand for John.

Now, we know that Christians throughout the ancient world were under terrific persecution, first from Jews who hated their new religion,[20] then from the Romans (cf. Eusebius' *Ecclesiastical History*). This is the historical backdrop to the last book of the Bible. With this thought in mind, Jay Adams calls the Revelation "a handbook for persecuted churches" (*Interpreting the Revelation*, 3 tape series). What he means is that John was writing a practical letter, though coded for

---

18. Rev. 22:10 reads, "Do not seal up the words of the prophecy of this book, for the time is *near.*"

19. Rome was not even a viable candidate for world supremacy when Daniel prophesied about this.

20. Observe the apostle Paul's drive to exterminate the church before his conversion; the book of Acts reveals continued sufferings: 14:5; 17:1-9; 21:27ff., etc.

secrecy, warning and comforting several strategic church congregations (chaps. 2, 3) along a postal route up through Asia Minor. We believe John was *not* prophesying about a distantly future series of events that would have no meaning to the assemblies receiving this Epistle.

So once again we cannot emphasize context strongly enough. McDowell writes, "We must take the trouble to learn as much as possible concerning the historical situation to which the book of Revelation belongs. It is only when this historical situation is reconstructed that Revelation comes alive and we are able to enter sympathetically into the mind and the heart of the author and his readers. Perhaps no other book of the Bible has suffered more from being wrenched from its historical context than has Revelation."[21] And we are in complete agreement. This is the key to proper interpretation, especially of such a book as this; if we take textual elements into consideration, we have put the right foot forward and taken a giant step toward understanding.

Whereas the comprehensivist branch of amilliennialism concurs that the messianic kingdom of Jesus Christ (the church) is one and the same as the thousand-year reign of Revelation 20, its exponents view most of this book (chaps. 2–19) as a metaphorical survey of history, in other words, the gospel age. They believe it signifies the spiritual tribulations which Christians will face throughout the entire period until the end. However, though we would agree that the church must contend against evil, we are not of the opinion that the Revelation deals wholly with this issue. We feel that the preterist interpretation best resolves the apparent mysteries in this inspired piece of apocalyptic literature.

According to this position, the outline of the Revelation would adhere to Jesus' own words in 1:19 as follows:

---

21. Edward A. McDowell, *The Meaning and Message of the Book of Revelation* (Nashville: Broadman Press, 1951), p. 1. All rights reserved. Used by permission.

I. Chapter 1, the things which *were:*
   A. Verses 1-8, introduction.
   B. Verses 9-20, figurative picture of the magnificent risen Lord.
II. Chapters 2–3, the things which *are* (John's contemporary situation among representative churches):
   A. Ephesus
   B. Smyrna
   C. Pergamum
   D. Thyatira
   E. Sardis
   F. Philadelphia
   G. Laodicea
III. Chapters 4–22, the things which *shall be:*
   A. *Shortly:* Chapters 4–20:6.
      1. Seals, trumpets, bowls: the story of persecution, judgment, and victory.
         a. Chapter 4, unveiling of the heavenly scene to encourage the saints, introduction of the plot and characters.
         b. Chapters 5–7, scroll with seven seals, an account of the judgments to come.
         c. Chapters 8–15, seven trumpets herald the agents who are to carry out the judgments revealed.
            1) Chapters 12–13, dragon and beasts.
            2) Chapters 14–15, visions.
         d. Chapter 16, seven bowls of wrath poured out, the actual perpetration of the judgments revealed.
      2. The church's enemies.
         a. Chapters 6–11, the church's first enemy, the Jew, is defeated, culminating in the destruction of Jerusalem.
         b. Chapter 12, a transition from the first to the second enemy of the church.
         c. Chapters 13–19, the church's second enemy, the Roman Empire, is defeated, represented in the destruction of the city of Rome.
      3. Chapter 20, a transition from the Jewish and Roman persecutions into the eternal state; verses 1-6 reveal the present-day kingdom of Christ, the gospel age.
   B. *At the end:* Chapter 20:7–Chapter 22.
      1. Chapter 20:7-15, final judgment.
      2. Chapers 21–22, new heavens, earth, Jerusalem: eternity.

So this is the scope of the Apocalypse, obscure only because of its imagery and dispensational presuppositions (noncontextual interpretation). Remember, most of the Revelation deals with the immediate future insofar as the author is concerned. It has to do with what the first-century church was about to encounter—persecution. It has to do with how God was going to deal with the situation, by passing judgment against the enemies inspired by the dragon, or the devil. It has to do with the establishment of the kingdom of Christ, who is to rule throughout the whole period when Satan is bound to deceive the gentile nations no more. It has to do with the end times, too, when Satan will be loosed again to deceive the peoples. And finally, it has to do with the devil's ultimate destruction at the end of this age, when eternity will be ushered in and new Jerusalem (heaven) is our abiding place with God.

Thus we see that the Revelation is not such a big mystery after all, not really. To declare as much is to refute the meaning of its name (an "unveiling") and to deny Scripture itself: "The Revelation . . . which God gave Him to *show* to His bond-servants . . . and He sent and *communicated* it by His angel to His bond-servant John" (Rev. 1:1).

15. But what about all the details of Revelation?

We have just presented a general background and outline to the book of Revelation in order to give you an overview for clearer understanding without getting bogged down in some of these details, which have historically thrown Christians off and which are definitely subject to opinion (among all eschatological schools of thought) because of their symbolic nature. Moreover, we feel they are relatively minor issues compared to some of the other topics to which we have devoted emphasis. Not only that, but they tend toward divisiveness, and considering their visionary character and the brevity of their exposure in God's Word, we believe they have been blown far out of proportion. The number of interpretations to these obscure images are as many as all the cults and sects that have derived from Christianity throughout history.

Nevertheless, they appear to be popular concerns which have captivated Christendom's imagination and caused quite a stir despite their relative insignificance, and so we thought we'd touch upon some of them briefly. Remember, please, that this is not an exegesis, an approach necessary for thorough answers.

The 24 Elders, chapters 4–5: The most common premillennial view of these 24 personages is that they depict the 12 tribes of Israel out of the Old Testament and the 12 apostles from the New Testament, thereby representing God's elect right through the entire Bible. In fact, this is not an unpopular position even among some nonmillenarians; it is tenable enough, but there is no proof. Scripture gives us very few clues, leading us to conclude that it isn't all that important an issue. Any conjecture one attempts in order to decipher their identity is bound to remain just that, pure speculation.

What really matters here is the role they play in the divine drama of Revelation. They are a part of the heavenly court scene and "are here to create the proper effect. Later in the book, they help carry the story forward, much as the chorus in a Greek tragedy (cf. chaps. 4, 5, 7, 11, 19)" (Jay Adams, *The Time Is at Hand,* p. 61).

The 144,000, chapter 7: The popular futurist view claims that these people are Jews who will be saved out of the great tribulation occurring just after the rapture. They will then go forth as witnesses of God to preach for seven years in a pagan world. Once again, the premillennialist prefers literalism to contextualism.

However, the amillennialist adopts either a spiritual interpretation (e.g., "symbolic of the new Israel that embraces men from every nation and race, people and tongue"; *New American Bible,* footnote on Rev. 7:4-8), or an historical one. We tend to consider the latter view as the most dependable.

Accordingly, during the fall of Jerusalem in A.D. 70, the Christian Jews, who had heard Jesus' words in Luke 21:20-24 and obeyed them, managed to escape the destruction that was to befall that city. Eusebius tells us (*Ecclesiastical History,* chap. 5) that not one Christian died in the flight to Pella across the Jordan. There is no question that the 144,000 are identified as Jews in the text, and history records that many thousands of refugees from the Jerusalem holocaust became witnesses in a gentile world for the gospel of Christ. The actual number "144,000" is, therefore, symbolic like most of the numerals in the Apocalypse.

The Two Witnesses, chapter 11: Opinions have proliferated on this question as well. Futurists insist that in the midst of the great tribulation to come, two men (often identified with Moses and Elijah, either in person or in character) will give witness to the truth. They will be slain, then restored to life. Once again, overliteralization gives rise to absurdity, especially when another interpretation is rational within the framework of natural biblical intent.

The idea of Moses and Elijah itself is not entirely implausible, but only as *types*, perhaps of the law and the prophets or of civil and religious government, since the Roman Empire was powerful enough to quash these two national characteristics of Israel during the period of her political subjugation to Rome (first century B.C. to fifth century A.D.). Nevertheless, these were destined to resurrection in the new Israel, the church of Jesus Christ.

Armageddon, chapter 16: This word actually means "mountain of Meggido," where many a battle was fought in the Old Testament (Judges 5:19ff.; II Kings 9:27; II Chron. 35:20-24). Because of this association with warfare, "Armageddon" has come to be a symbol for the ultimate battle between good and evil at the end of the world.

Premillennialists believe physical combat will actually take place at the completion of the millennial reign, after Satan has once again been loosed; the location will be near Meggido, in the valley of Jezreel, located in northern Israel. Jesus and His heavenly forces (saints and angels) will be victorious to the uttermost.

But we take Armageddon to represent no more than God's judgment upon the city of Rome and the empire of Rome in their historical settings. However, Revelation 20:7-10 does speak of a final battle between God and Satan,[22] symbolizing the triumph of good over evil which will happen at the great day of the Lord. The reason for confusion here is that futurists have borrowed the name "Armageddon" from the sixteenth chapter and have applied it to an unrelated text in the twentieth chapter.

The Ten Horns of the Beast, chapter 17: The standard dispensational position is that these ten horns depict the restored Roman Empire, sometimes equated with today's Common Market of Europe. It identifies them with Daniel's "ten" toes of the statue in Nebuchadnezzar's dream (Dan. 2:41), a prophetic reference to the Roman Empire of Jesus' time. As usual, they not only yank Revelation 17 out of context, but they put far more meaning (according to a preconceived, well-established theological scheme) into the passage in question than is justifiable.

What then might these ten horns mean within the scope of the verses preceding and following? Let's put this vision within John's contemporary scene, since the angel himself explains what it is in contemporary

---

22. Please see the discussion to follow shortly on Gog and Magog.

language. These ten horns sit upon the seven heads of one beast, which is the fourth beast of Daniel (7:7), representing the Roman Empire. The seven heads are obviously the Seven Hills of Rome, and the ten horns likely symbolize provincial governors of the ten Roman provinces in Asia Minor, whose authority went to Rome the suppressor. But this prophecy is more involved than that. Suffice it to say that (1) the harlot (17:5), another ingredient in this text, is the *city* of Rome, (2) the beast is the *empire* of Rome as typified in Nero,[23] and (3) the horns constitute the vassal government who, along with Rome, persecuted the Christian community, but who ultimately turned against Rome.

What is important in this case is the chronology of the scene as opposed to the identification of the characters. The situation has already occurred in ancient history; the beast is an empire which *was,* not which will be. It existed at the time of John's writing the Revelation. The Bible simply does not teach that the Roman Empire must be restored. As Adams puts it, "How artificial to suppose that at a time yet future, a revived Roman empire will again destroy a restored and rebuilt Jewish temple—exactly as in 70 A.D." *(The Time Is at Hand,* p. 70).

Gog and Magog, chapter 20: The actual names Gog and Magog (meaning "land of Gog") are taken from Ezekiel (chaps. 38, 39), who was prophesying about specific persons and nations which were to arrive on the scene a few centuries later. Other names in this Old Testament passage (Meshach, Tubal, Gomer, Beth-togarmah) have been applied by futurists to modern states, but since such nations existed in Ezekiel's day around the Black Sea, it is more reasonable to conclude that this prophet was the bearer of God's message for a generation closer to his own. For instance, Boersma sees fulfillment of Ezekiel's prediction in God's protection of Israel in the time of the Maccabees against Antiochus Epiphanes (second century B.C.). Indeed, the facts are the same.

Nevertheless, because the book of Ezekiel has many apocalyptic characteristics, these utterances may have a second, more symbolic application. Some amillennialists like Boersma take the comprehensivist approach, applying Satan's influence over Gog and Magog spiritually to mean the battle we have as Christians against wickedness all our lives

---

23. Legend had it that Nero would return from the dead, and he did come to life again in a sense through the evil traits of Domitian. Hence, references to his resurrection: Rev. 13:3, 14; 17:8, 11.

long. For them, God's victory over Gog and Magog portrays His protection for us when we face the warfare against the world and the flesh and the devil.

But our feeling is that, instead of hordes from the North (Russia, Germany, etc.) coming down in full vengeance on the little nation of Israel some day hence, playing a role in the apocalyptic "Battle of Armageddon" (Rev. 16), as some premillennialists say, Gog and Magog depict all the gentile pagan nations whom Satan beguiles and leads in final conflict against God, a *spiritual* conflict for the most part, but which could be manifested in physical warfare, wherein the devil (with all evil) is defeated by the return of Jesus Christ in judgment, when the earth will be burned up (II Pet. 3:10) and a new heaven and a new earth will replace the present order.

16. Isn't there a difference between the Day of the Lord and the Day of Christ?

No, but dispensationalists insist on a distinction. Many of them assert that the day of Christ will occur first (at the rapture, which will be "secret," only for believers), that it always indicates blessing for the saints, and that it encompasses the idea of the Greek word *parousia* (or "presence," "arrival"). On the other hand, the day of the Lord will take place at the close of the great tribulation, implies judgment for nonbelievers, and is equated with *apokalupsis* (or "unveiling," "revelation"). In point of fact, though, these two days (and the Greek terms) are identical.

In Matthew 24:37-39, *parousia* is used of judgment (like Noah's flood), while I Corinthians 1:7 and II Thessalonians 1:7 employ *apokalupsis* in reference to a blessing upon the saints. There are other examples in New Testament writings, as well, that reverse the dispensational distinction: Luke 17 (vv. 24, 26, 30) seems to assert that the day of Christ ("the day of the Son of Man") will bring destruction, whereas II Peter 3:12 encourages believers to look for the hastening of the day of the Lord ("the day of God"), a very positive statement.

Furthermore, a number of New Testament passages employ *parousia* in a more general way, indicating the second advent without specific reference to the rapture. In fact, according to dispensational theology, *apokalupsis* would have been the more appropriate word (e.g., I Thess. 3:13; II Pet. 1:16). And at times *parousia* is used in connection with other New Testament characters, thereby having no eschatological significance whatsoever; see Matthew 26:50, where it refers to Judas, Luke 13:1 for "some present," Philippians 1:26 concerning Paul, etc. Likewise, *apokalupsis* sometimes deals with the second advent only (I Pet. 1:7, 13) or persons and contexts with noneschatological implication: Matthew 11:25; Luke 2:35; Ephesians 3:5; Romans 1:17, 18, and so forth.

It is interesting, too, that there is yet a third Greek word for "coming" which has to do with the second advent: *epiphaneia* (or "show"); II Timothy 4:8 and Titus 2:13 indicate blessing, while II Timothy 4:1 speaks of judgment. To complicate matters further, another Greek verb (*erchomai*) can mean "come" or "go," but its emphasis is *motion*. It is not one of the three New Testament verbs that describe Christ's return. For example, as mentioned in our discussion on the Olivet Discourse, *erchomai* depicts Jesus as moving in the clouds (Matt. 24:30; Mark 13:26; Luke 21:27), having to do with His ascension (Dan. 7:13), not His second coming.

We've already alluded to the universal characteristics of language and to the difficulties inherent in translation. Here is another good illustration of the confusion we get ourselves into when we divide God's Word into a noncontextual scheme of theology. If in English we can use many words to mean the second advent (Christ's "arrival," the "unveiling" of His power, Jesus will "show" Himself, among others), why do we put unnatural linguistic restrictions on Greek? It is most logical to conclude that the New Testament writers employed *parousia, apokalupsis,* and *epiphaneia* as synonyms for that great day of God our Savior Jesus Christ.

And it is really preposterous to make a distinction between two words ("Christ" and "Lord") when Scripture links them so often: "God has made Him both *Lord* and *Christ*—this Jesus whom you crucified" (Acts 2:36). See also Luke 2:11 and Philippians 2:11.

Moreover, it is important to keep in mind that the Bible stresses the surprise aspect of Jesus' second coming (I Thess. 5:3). If the "secret rapture" of the day of Christ is true, then the day of the Lord exactly seven years following could hardly be unexpected. This is contrary to all

New Testament teaching on the second coming.

Thus we see that instead of two separate phases to our Lord's return (or a duplication of this event), the day of Christ and the day of the Lord are one and the same.[24] Grier sums up this discussion well for us: "Now, we will make bold to say that all efforts to distinguish these terms—'coming,' 'revelation,' 'day of Christ,' and 'day of the Lord'—have failed and are bound to fail. These terms are really interchangeable, and refer one and all to the great epochal event at the end of the world, when Christ will come to bless and reward His people, and to judge the world in righteousness."[25]

17. What is in store for the future according to amillennialism?

Unlike the pretribulation futurist, the amillennialist does not believe there will be *two* second advents of our Lord (to repeat: one at the "secret rapture," when Jesus will appear to take His own to be with Him, and the second at the time of His physical reign in an earthly Jerusalem). We believe rather in a simultaneous physical resurrection of both the "saved" and the "lost" (John 5:28, 29), which is to occur at the culmination of this age, when we move directly through the last judgment into the eternal state, all of which constitutes a single second coming. After all, our Lord's interpretation of the parable of the wheat and the tares (Matt. 13:24-43) indicates that the Lord will take the ungodly at the same time as the godly, and Matthew 25:31ff. affirms that the sheep (Christians) will be judged simultaneously with the goats (non-Christians). And again, in order to maintain the "surprise element" of Jesus' return, we must consider it as a single event; otherwise we could calculate to the minute when He would appear, seeing that the "rapture" is considered to be exactly seven years prior to the establishment of the "millennium."

---

24. Note that the amillennial position does *not* teach a "spiritualized" second coming, as is charged by some Bible teachers, both premillennial and postmillennial (e.g., George E. Ladd in *Jesus and the Kingdom,* and Val. J. Sauer Jr. in *The Eschatology Handbook*). This is exactly wrong. We believe firmly in a literal (physical) second coming.

25. W. J. Grier, *The Momentous Event* (Carlisle, Pa.: The Banner of Truth Trust, 1945), p. 60.

As regards national Israel, that is, her state and government and country, she plays virtually no more role in fulfillment of prophecy, either from the Old Testament or from the New. This view is, of course, at odds with our dispensational brothers. The premillenarian L. S. Chafer says that not only will Israel again gather within the Palestinian borders, but that Judaism will be restored. He also believes there will be two distinct peoples in God's plan: an earthly people inhabiting the world into eternity and a heavenly people inhabiting paradise with God forever. As Grier puts it, "This may be consistent literalism, but surely it is a veritable delirium of folly. The literalism which insists on the Old Testament prophecies being referred to the Israel after the flesh, is utterly inconsistent with the universal New Testament application of the promises to the spiritual seed."[26]

Both William Sanday and Arthur Headlam identify the term "Israel" as used in the New Testament with the body of Christians, as in Galatians 6:16, which reads, "And those who will walk by this rule, peace and mercy be upon them, and upon the Israel of God." The context demands that we interpret "Israel" to mean the Christian church, underscoring a basic amillennial doctrine noted often in this treatise. Even a classical premillennialist like George Ladd concurs, as follows: "Hebrews flatly affirms that the whole Mosaic system is obsolete and about to pass away. Therefore the popular Dispensational position that Israel is the 'clock of prophecy' is misguided" (*The Last Things,* p. 28). C. K. Lehman as well: "There are no unfulfilled prophecies concerning Christ or Israel which are not comprehended under the New Covenant" (*The Fulfillment of Prophecy,* p. 12).

Even the recent (1948) reestablishment of Israel as a sovereign nation and the 1967 "Six Day War" (where the Jewish state once again gained control over Jerusalem) have nothing to do with eschatology, because the church has inherited Israel's birthright, as we have seen (Matt. 8:10-12), thereby becoming God's instrument for salvation in the New Testament age, as opposed to the Jews in the Old.

Nevertheless, Romans 11:25 indicates that there may yet be one more prophecy regarding the Jewish *race* that must come to pass before the end: when the "time of the Gentiles" is completed, it appears that God will open the Hebrew heart to the Messiah. This could be understood in

26. W. J. Grier, *The Momentous Event* (Carlisle, Pa.: The Banner of Truth Trust, 1945), p. 50.

connection with the loosing of Satan (Rev. 20:3) to blind the gentile nations once more from the gospel of truth before the Lord's return, a reversal of spiritual polarization, you might say. With this in mind, it may well follow that Israel "after the flesh," now in a period of darkness because of her rejection of Jesus, might be freed to perceive the message of the cross and "be grafted back" where she had been "cut off" (Rom. 11:24).

Not all amillennialists are in full agreement on this issue, however. Concerning Romans 11, Anthony Hoekema believes there is nothing in store specifically for the Jew, either as a race or as a nation; as individuals, though, some will become part of the church throughout the gospel age. And while William Hendriksen and Louis Berkhof understand this chapter in the light of "spiritual Israel," or the church, Boersma interprets it historically, that is, in the context of the apostle Paul's own day. Finally, Adams, Grier, and Vos concur for the most part with our stand that conversions among the Jews will increase dramatically at the time near the end. Romans 11:26 puts it all together, declaring that "all Israel will be saved" and signifying the full measure of God's elect out of both Jewish and gentile humanity.

However, the return of the Jews from around the world to the land of Palestine should not be mistaken for spiritual revival! There may be a time of faith renewal among the Hebrews, but restoration to their land has nothing to do with it. So Grier points out: "Is it proper to hail the return of unconverted, rebellious Jews to Palestine as a fulfilment of prophecy? It would not seem to be so, for prophecy closely links the ideas of *conversion* and 'restoration' (Deut. 30:8-10; Ezek. 20:38)."[27]

And certainly the reinstatement of the Jewish people in the land of Israel is *not* a spiritual event. It is apparent that the collective Israeli heart is bound and determined to reject Jesus as Messiah—still. But when the time of the Gentiles is accomplished, this attitude will change and many a Jew will turn to the Lord, saved not through any divine cataclysmic intervention or by reestablished Judaic sacrifice, but through the blood of the Lamb of God.

Even so, it is true today that the individual Jew can enter the kingdom of Christ, but he does so by faith in our Savior Jesus. Believing Jews do not go by a different set of rules. The Messiah is the only door, the only

---

27. W. J. Grier, *The Momentous Event* (Carlisle, Pa.: The Banner of Truth Trust, 1945), p. 123, italics ours.

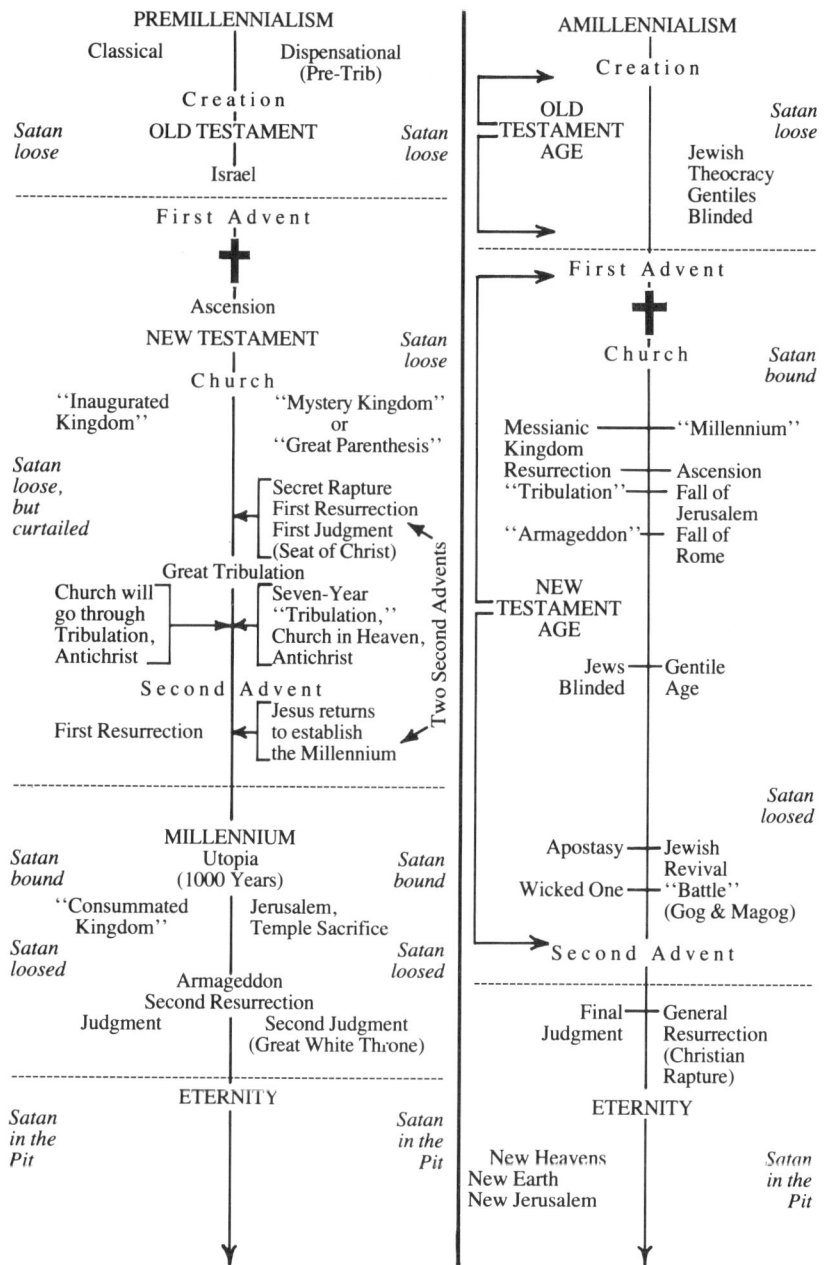

way. He always will be—for anyone and everyone, Jew or Gentile. The wall of separation has been torn down (Eph. 2:14).

On a more general note, the preceding charts may help you see at a glance what it is that these two schools of eschatological thought believe is yet in store for the future. (We have diagrammed both the classical and the dispensational views of premillennialism, but only the preterist view of amillennialism, not the comprehensivist. Postmillennialism is not set forth here for comparison, either.)

18. Where did the whole system of premillennialism come from?

We've talked about the Jewish two-age hope, as well as a tendency to hyperliteralize, and these are two of the sources for the premillennial error. However, there are likely any number of roots, one of which seems to stand above the others: a basic misconception of the "two" resurrections (and the "two" deaths) in Revelation 20:5-6. As illustrated in the preceding diagram, the premillennialist believes there will be one resurrection of the righteous (Christians) before the thousand-year millennium, followed by a second resurrection (and a second judgment, according to dispensationalists) of the unrighteous (non-Christians) at the end of the thousand years. The "first resurrection," then, allows for the saints to rule with Jesus in Jerusalem. (Both of these resurrections are to be physical, by the way.) Because of this interpretation, the premillennialist sees validity in the belief that there will be an interregnum, a future millennium.

In light of other Scriptures, as we will show, the present writers find it hard to justify such an inference. B. B. Warfield concurs: "John [the divine] knows no more of two [physical] resurrections—of the saints and of the wicked—than does Paul: and the whole theory of an intervening millennium . . . goes up in smoke" (*Biblical Doctrines*, p. 661). So even Revelation doesn't substantiate the premillennial position.

Because of words in the Apocalypse like "martyred" and "beheaded" with reference to the saints, some commentators have concluded that *physical* death is implied. This is not an exclusively premillenarian position, either. The preterist Jay Adams is of this opinion, holding that it is those believers who suffered martyrdom during the first century who now reign with our Lord in heaven. Others take a broader view, but still limit the "first resurrection" to the consequence of bodily death: it is those who have experienced the new birth during their lifetimes who will undergo the "first resurrection" when they die to this biological existence and their souls are raised to heaven, where they then rule with Jesus over the spiritual dominion called the church.

Nevertheless, it is our conviction that Augustinian theology stands correct: the first resurrection constitutes a purely spiritual event, the new birth into God's kingdom while on earth, where the church militant reigns, along with the church triumphant in Glory. Galatians 2:20 testifies to this: "I [Paul] am crucified with Christ: nevertheless I live; yet not I, but Christ liveth in me" (King James Version). As Christians, we have been granted authority over sin while yet in our weak flesh (cf. Matt. 28:18-20; John 1:12; John 14:12); we don't have to wait for the next life to exercise this God-given power. With regards to Ephesians 2:4-6, F. J. Huegel writes, "Here we have the amazing declaration of the inspired Word of God to the effect that the Christian sits where Jesus sits, that he actually shares, though it be only in spirit (there is nothing so real as spirit) his Saviour's very throne" (*Reigning with Christ,* p. 41).[28]

Therefore, when an obscure and involved text like Revelation 20 is studied in conjunction with far more direct teaching passages, its meaning becomes clear. For instance, Jesus speaks of two resurrections in John 5:24-29, where He says that whoever hears His words and believes on the Father who sent Him has passed out of *death* into *life:* a resurrection, to put it another way. He goes on to say the hour "now is" when the dead who hear His voice will live. This we take to be the *true* first resurrection; it is the new birth. "The first resurrection is to be understood spiritually as birth into the life of grace. . . . The image [of the thrones in Rev. 20:4] intends to show the greatness of the Christian, already beginning to reign with Christ. . . . Those who take part in the first resurrection are not injured by the second death which is defined in 20:14 . . ." (J. M. Ford, *Revelation,* p. 351). What could this mean but that the Christian need not fear the perpetual "death" of separation from his God in eternity!

Then Jesus goes on (John 5:28-29) to discuss another kind of resurrection. He says that the time is coming when everyone will hear His voice

---

28. Reprinted by permission from *Reigning With Christ,* by F. J. Huegel, published and copyrighted 1963, Bethany Fellowship, Inc., Minneapolis, Minn.

while yet they are "in the tombs," and they will "come forth" either to life (those "who have done good") or to judgment (those "who have done evil"). This clearly is a physical resurrection; it is general (both Christians and non-Christians); and it is future. We surely can be grateful that this text from our Lord's own lips is so succinct and unencumbered, in order that we can comprehend without doubt what the "two resurrections" of Revelation 20 constitute.

It is even more fortunate that God saw fit to supply us with further Bible information on this topic. Perhaps another of the best examples is the parable of the wheat and the tares in Matthew 13:24-30, 34-43, alluded to earlier in a related context. The landowner in this story advises that both the wheat and the tares (weeds) be allowed to "grow together until the harvest," at which time the tares are to be collected first, followed immediately by the gathering of the wheat. Jesus Himself proceeds to give the explanation of the parable: the angels would come and snatch the wicked from the righteous "at the end of the age."[29] Christ is saying here that there will be only one physical resurrection at the end. Then He goes on to describe one judgment.

Other Scripture references corroborate this. None of them speaks of physical resurrections (plural) as though there are more than one (e.g., Acts 24:15), and many of them deal with only one *kind* of resurrection at a time, either spiritual or bodily. (Matt. 22:30 and John 11:24, for example. Note in the latter verse that even the righteous will be raised on the last day, not a physical resurrection *before* the millennium.) And the fact that a particular text may deal with only one resurrection proves only that the lesson is directed at the topic in question, not that there are two physical resurrections separated by a thousand years.

Likewise regarding the final judgment, there will be only one, wherein God reveals the destinies of all mankind, both the just and the unjust (Matt. 16:27). There will not be a distinct "judgment seat of Christ" for believers before the "millennium" and another called the "great white throne (judgment)" for unbelievers afterwards, as some premillennialists assert. The Bible simply does not teach this. Rather, it states that we will *all* stand before the judgment seat of God (Rom. 14:10). And again, Matthew 25:32 tells us that the sheep (the righteous) will be divided from the goats (the unrighteous) at one and the same time.

---

29. Note that the wicked are gathered out of *Christ's* kingdom and the righteous are delivered into the *Father's* kingdom (Matt. 13:41, 43; cf. I Cor. 15:24).

H. H. Halley has put it thus: "The Judgment will be complete. Every person from every age and nation will be there. . . . It will be the 'Day when God shall Judge the Secrets of men,' spoken of by Paul in Rom. 2:16. There will be only two classes: the Saved and the Lost" (*Halley's Bible Handbook,* p. 670).[30]

Getting back to Revelation 20, it is interesting that the text doesn't even mention a "second resurrection," nor does it speak of a "first death"; they have been interpolated. (This isn't to say they are not implied, however.) At any rate, we understand these terms as follows: (1) the "first resurrection" is spiritual, present, and limited to believers (the new birth); (2) the "second resurrection" is physical, future, and general (for all men of all ages, whether believers or not); (3) the "first death" is physical, present, and general (the biological termination of life common to all flesh); and (4) the "second death" is spiritual, future, and limited to non-Christians: eternal separation from God (hell).

19. Isn't all this just academic? Or does it really make a difference in everyday life which view we adopt?

We believe it does make a difference—in inner attitude to begin with. The futurist approach tends to quench one's interest in the kingdom promises: if everything is way off in the future somewhere, why bother about it at all, much less examine it closely. How often have we heard this! But to repeat, we should not think of amillennialism as just another branch of eschatology (the study of *final* things), but rather as the study of the *here* and *now.* Knowing that the promised kingdom which Jesus preached so fervently is with us today can transform us into citizens more aware of our authority as reigning with the Lord Jesus. Even though premillennialists would claim authority as Christians, their constant meditation on the arrival of the future millennium betrays a lack of appreciation for this age, in which the Holy Spirit dwells with power. This is especially true of dispensationalism; the classical branch is guilty to a lesser degree.

Evidently it was vitally important to Jesus Himself that the Jews of his

---

30. Copyright © 1965 by Halley's Bible Handbook, Ind. Reprinted by permission.

day apprehend exactly what kind of kingdom it was that He was offering them. He went to great pains to reiterate the nature of His messiahship in word (Matt. 28:18; Luke 17:21; John 18:36, etc.), to demonstrate it in action (Matt. 18:1-6; Luke 7:20-22; 11:14, 20, etc.), and to illustrate it in parables (Matt. 13:45-46; Luke 8:4-15; 14:15-24, etc.). Some have argued that these "kingdom parables" portray a future millennium, but this is entirely wrong. Jesus spoke to the concerns of His contemporaries—including us, because our Lord is alive today! His teaching was practical: the ethics of the church, His kingdom.[31]

Everywhere He went and whenever He could, Jesus "preached the kingdom," a synonym for salvation. No amount of social pressure would make Him budge from His "brand" of messianism, because it was the truth. He held His position even to the point of rejection by the "chosen people," who refused to accept His "interpretation" of what God's kingdom was all about. If it was critical to our Lord back then, surely it is still vital to Him that we (His present "chosen people") should understand His message of the kingdom. And if it's important to Jesus, it ought to be important to us.

But we get even more out of amillennialism. A new, less complicated perception of the whole of God's Word (His plan, His mind) opens up to us. The futurist theology of even some very well-known Bible teachers can become extremely confusing and therefore unnecessarily complex. Their thinking would be called "duplistic" (or double), with a great deal of overlap and repeated concepts, doubling up on prophecy, creating conditions a second time for fufillment already accomplished.

We would refer you to the above charts for an excellent example: the futurists really believe in *two* second advents, or at least two phases of a single second advent. But such a view is entirely unscriptural. In his own scholarly fashion, Geerhardus Vos is emphatic about the apostle Paul's eschatology: "The parousia taken as an event is with Paul catastrophic. Of a development [i.e., stages or phases] within the limits of the concept, or a duplication or triplication of the event there is nowhere any trace. It is a point of eventuation [i.e., the beginning of the end], not a series of successive events" (*The Pauline Eschatology,* p. 76). And what Vos says here of Paul's writings we would apply to all biblical eschatology. Hoekema concurs: "The Amillennialist understands the Second Coming

31. Cf. C. H. Dodd's *The Parables of the Kingdom,* R. Mufmord's *The King and You,* and J. Sanford's *The Kingdom Within.*

of Christ to be a single event, not one that involves two phases" (*The Bible and the Future,* p. 174).

Furthermore, Lindsey, Darby, Scofield, Pentecost, and other premillenarians all believe in one way or another that the ancient Roman Empire must be reinstituted in order to set up the right circumstances for completion of prophecy. Some go so far as to recognize that Nero probably fulfilled the beast prediction in the first century, but they insist there will have to be yet another just like Nero later on, near the end. "There is little doubt," Barclay writes, "that the number of the beast stands for Nero; and that John in it is forecasting the coming of Antichrist in the form of Nero, the incarnation of all evil, returning to this world" (*The Revelation of John,* 2:133). He believes this in spite of the fact that the original Nero fulfilled the prophecy satisfactorily in every way.

This kind of duplistic thinking happens over and over in most premillennial theology. Even the kingdom of the Son is doubled up: the present "mystery kingdom" or "inaugurated kingdom," followed by its culmination in an earthly millennial reign of Christ. But only *one* kingdom was prophesied (Dan. 2:44; Heb. 12:28). To deny the presence of Christ's messianic kingdom is to deny that Jesus was the Messiah! It's as serious as that. Dispensationalists are quick to agree that we Christians are part of some vague sort of kingdom about the face of the earth today, but they don't know what it is because they say it wasn't foretold in the Old Testament—this, the very church of God! Whatever kind of kingdom we have now, they won't call it the "millennium" or the "messianic kingdom," which must appear after the second advent, they maintain, a *second* kingdom of Christ.

But most blatant of all, premillennialism (as it is popularly conceived today in dispensationalism) is heretical doctrine in that it demands reinstitution (duplicity again) of the sacrificial system with the rebuilding of the temple during the future millennium. This belief mocks the cross by making it insufficient. Whatever could be the purpose of sacrificing animals all over again as was practiced in the Old Testament, when Jesus offered Himself once for all (Heb. 10:12) and when the blood of animals avails nothing (Heb. 10:4)? The Old Testament sacrifices were but shadows to be fulfilled in the reality of the cross (Heb. 8:5-6). Indeed, our Lord's death put an end to all the Mosaic system! After all, His priesthood according to Melchizedek's order is greater than Aaron's; it is eternal, perpetual (Heb. 7:17). And remember, the Father Himself showed divine disapproval of continued sacrifice when He tore the temple veil in two. In his *Momentous Event*[32] Grier quotes Douglas's *Structure of Prophecy* in this regard: "A temple with sacrifices now would be the most daring denial of the all-sufficiency of the sacrifice of Christ, and of the efficacy of the blood of His atonement. He who sacrificed before, confessed the Messiah; he who should sacrifice now, would most solemnly and sacrilegiously deny Him." Amen!

In addition, we would repeat that a persistently futurist view of Scripture tends to deprecate what God has given us today. To seek for something "better" yet to come is to overlook "these last days" when God has spoken to us through the best, His very Son (Heb. 1:2). We don't have to look to the East, go to Jerusalem, sacrifice an animal, depend on the high priest to enter the Holy of Holies for us, but rather we can do these things ourselves through the power of the Holy Spirit dwelling in our hearts—anytime, anywhere. Huegel can hardly put the believer's blessed state into words: "The Christian's position is of such a glorious nature as to beggar all description. He has been literally, actually, really enthroned in spirit with Christ his Lord. When he accepts this fact by faith, the Holy Spirit makes it a reality in experience and he begins to reign in life, by one, even Jesus (Romans 5:17)" (*Reigning with Christ*, p. 43).[33]

Any dispensational repudiation of the messianic significance in today's church can be vividly demonstrated by remarks the present writers have heard from premillennialists. Upon first hearing that the millennium is none other than the church, they have exclaimed, "If *this* is the millennium, then we're *really* disappointed!" They've missed the whole point of Christian reality in search of a Jewish dream. Instead of the transcendent "delicacies" of communion with the Paraclete (the Comforter), they concentrate on the bodily presence of Jesus in national Israel (John 16:7); they complain that the power of the Holy Spirit in the gospel of God "to will and to work for His good pleasure" (Phil. 2:13) isn't enough, so they invent Satan's total subjugation (James 4:7); they prefer a physical temple in geographical Jerusalem to the *kodesh kodashim* (Holy of Holies) in the very heart of every Christian (I Cor. 3:16). To

---

32. From W. J. Grier, *The Momentous Event* (Carlisle, Pa.: The Banner of Truth Trust, 1945), p. 38.

33. Reprinted by permission from *Reigning With Christ* by F. J. Huegel, published and copyrighted 1963, Bethany Fellowship, Inc., Minneapolis, Minn.

desire the material over the spiritual is flagrantly contrary to the entire thrust of Jesus' teaching, contrary to the very core of biblical revelation, both Old and New Testaments.

Because of this kind of postponement-mentality, the gospel of salvation is being preached from our pulpits without the gospel of the kingdom. But we should be telling the church world that their Savior is fully king, enthroned even today at the right hand of power (Luke 22:69), that He sits in glory as ruler of the kings on the earth (Rev. 1:5). Failing to do so, we deny our Lord the praise due Him for this wondrous kingdom He's bestowed upon us.

If only the Old Testament saints could hear what we hear and see what we see! Their vague hopes have been perfected in the abundant multiplicity of blessings in the kingdom of Christ. What unfathomable gifts! Oh what an unspeakable privilege to claim what the Son has accomplished for us and in us, His nation of priests (I Pet. 2:5)! God forbid that we should cling to the inferior, when He has given Himself once for all at the consummation of the ages! If this isn't an important distinction, we don't know what is.

20. How about a definition? What are the main features which characterize amillennialism?

We've used the word "amillennialism" so much in context that you probably have a very good idea of what it signifies already, but let's look at its linguistic roots for more information. The prefix "a" simply means "not" or "none" or "no," and so the principal idea is negative: what follows doesn't exist. Thus, technically, amillennialism implies that there is no millennium, nor will there be one at any time. However, some amillennial scholars don't want to go that far. They think the word tends to emphasize the negative unnecessarily. Jay Adams, for instance, prefers the term "realized millennialism," meaning that, yes, we believe in the "millennium," but not the way it is popularly conceived, both as to its character and its time of fulfillment. Still others like A. A. Hoekema don't mind making it perfectly clear that they reject any hint of a "millennium" whatsoever because it has been made to bear too strong a futurist and utopian stamp, not to mention dispensational. These call themselves "nonmillennialists," a word that more vividly describes their view to lay people.

The present writers wouldn't mind adopting the name "realized millennialism," but *only* if the nature and chronology of the millennium are clearly understood as spiritual and present; in other words, that it is identical with Christ's church prophesied in the Old Testament. However, because the term "millennium" is so fraught with preconceptions and misconceptions, and because such error is practically impossible to erase from the collective mind of any group, perhaps it would be wise to drop the word (or any derivative thereof) altogether from the name. This would be difficult but shouldn't be painful, since "millennium" appears nowhere in the Bible. And it would eliminate the eschatological flavor or influence in the word, to boot. But we have and make no suggestions; the *kingdom of Christ* is a glorious enough name!

As we have seen, the amillennialist believes that the millennium is the kingdom prophesied in Daniel 2:44 (cf. v. 35c), where the Lord God promised to establish an empire that would never end and that would embrace all the ends of the earth. We believe this dominion was realized by the crucifixion/resurrection at the ascension; Jesus took the spiritual throne of David at that time, as Scripture teaches: "God had sworn to him [David] . . . to seat one of his descendants [Jesus] upon his throne . . . [David] spoke of the resurrection of the Christ" (Acts 2:30-31).

And as we have made clear, we take that empire to be the church, an incorporeal kingdom of saints ruling with Jesus over the power of sin by the authority granted us from the Son through our faith in Him. When Christ returns to take us with Him to heaven, the "millennium" will cease and the kingdom of God moves into eternity. The Son has triumphed over the enemy; He was made victorious at the resurrection; He has caused us to be conquerors; He is preparing the kingdom as a bride without spot or wrinkle, anticipating the Father's reign.

Since we're dealing with extended definitions here, we might as well include the other eschatological positions, too. As you know by now, premillennialists hold that the millennium is yet future, and most say it is to be an earthly kingdom set up in temporal Israel with Jesus on David's literal throne in Jerusalem and with us ruling alongside Him there. (Other futurists claim that only Jews will reign with the Lord, while gentile saints remain in heaven.) Though physical, the millennium will be a government of justice and peace, where the world will reap the benefits, both tangible and intangible, of the pure reign of Christ. This "messianic kingdom" is to be exactly a thousand years long, but believers (or just the Jews, depending on the view) are to live the whole while, though unbelievers will go on giving birth and dying. Because Satan will be totally bound, there will be no real sin influence; thus will it be a perfect existence, a utopia. Preceding this millennium, Jesus will return to take His people with Him either before, in the middle of, or at the end of a seven-year period of supernaturally evil horror (the great tribulation); the time of its occurrence depends on the school of thought (pre-trib, mid-trib, or post-trib). When the seven years are up, Jesus is to come back once more, this time to set up the righteous domain just described, headquartered in Jerusalem. When the millennium itself is completed, Jesus is to lead us in victorious battle (Armageddon) against the devil and all his wicked forces. Then comes the final judgment (the great white throne judgment for the wicked, Christ's judgment seat for the righteous having already occurred a thousand years earlier); eternity ultimately follows.

By way of parenthesis, we draw your attention to a comparative analysis of these two views. We feel amillennialism is far more responsible because it is based on the spiritual substance of Scripture, whereas premillennialism becomes no less than a hodgepodge of fine points because its premise is arbitrary speculation, an extrabiblical system. You see, although the premillenarian claims stricter literalism for his hermeneutic (as if such an approach is always preferable), the amillennialist studies the Bible more contextually. The former tends to launch away from the text into his intricately detailed scheme of eschatology. We are persuaded that this is a very dangerous route. Perhaps the most important aspect of Bible study is context; the verses preceding and following a given passage supply many clues to its meaning. If one heeds the line of reasoning of the *whole,* he will more probably comprehend the *part,* even—and especially—when it is obscure.

Postmillennialists insist they differ from both the premillennial and the amillennial positions, but in actuality postmillennialism bears some definite similarities to each of these views. Whereas they believe the millennium is yet future and utopian (as held by premillennialists), they stress the spiritual renewal of God's people which will introduce the millennium, at the end of which Jesus returns (as taught in amillennialism). As noted earlier, though, this philosophy lost much of its popularity during the late nineteenth century, but some sincere scholars still adhere to it today.

Concluding Remarks

Juan Carlos Ortiz expresses his thoughts on the kingdom of God with such fresh excitement that we felt we could summarize our ideas in no better way than by sharing some of what he says:

> It's not easy to pass from one kingdom to the other, because these two kingdoms [the kingdom of God and the kingdom of darkness] are completely different and are at war. . . . Actually, Satan will never grant you a passport to go to the kingdom of God, but even if he would, in the kingdom of God they don't accept immigrants or tourists. You have to be born there. . . . And here is the message of the gospel, really: you cannot get into the kingdom of darkness unless you die; and you cannot get into the kingdom of God unless you are born there. We cannot do this. . . . Jesus came and solved this situation, providing us with a death and a new birth. . . . And this is what the cross is all about. The cross is Christ providing us with a death we were desperately needing. Jesus Christ did not die on the cross for Himself; He did not need to die for Himself. . . . He died to put in our hands a death by which we could be delivered from the kingdom of darkness. He provided a death to us and He provided a resurrection, a new starting, a new birth. . . . When Jesus rose from the dead, He rose [*sic*] us with Him, too. And we are born again, and when we are born, we are born into the kingdom of God (transcribed from an unpublished address delivered in Redwood City, Calif., July 2, 1978).

It is our belief that the major thrust of the Old Testament is to typify the coming Messiah (e.g., Joseph, Moses, Joshua, David) and to prophesy about His kingdom of righteousness (e.g., Psalms, Isaiah, Daniel, Zechariah). And likewise, the principal theme in the New Testament is the accomplishment of this messianism in Jesus Christ and the actual establishment of His promised kingdom by salvation at the completion of His visitation. Jesus affirms this when (in reply to the Sanhedrin's query regarding His mission) He claimed, "From now on the Son of Man will be seated at the right hand of the power of God" (Luke 22:69).

Before winding up, we'd like to add one more thought. There need be no fear in adopting the amillennial position. Besides the fact that it is historically orthodox and that its standard is God's Word, it doesn't alter the chief doctrines of the Christian faith the way premillennialism can.[34] The tenets of Scripture won't crumble under amillennialism; rather, they blossom when studied in the light of this realized system of theology. The sovereignty of God, salvation by grace, the cross, the resurrection, the virgin birth, Christian sanctification, the deity of Jesus Christ, all these remain rock solid. Indeed, such glorious truths are intensified!

* * * * * * *

We've presented this treatise as lay persons for lay persons, because it is our firm conviction that the laity has been persuaded, either consciously or subconsciously, to believe that the study of "doctrine" should be limited to the clergy, seminary students and professors, theologians—the Christian "elite." But we would adamantly declare otherwise! Since so much of the New Testament is doctrine, God must have intended that every one of us be schooled in it. We must get past the "pure milk of the word" (I Pet. 2:2) into the "solid food" (Heb. 5:12), the deeper principles of the Christian faith. "Be diligent to present yourself approved to God as a workman who does not need to be ashamed, *handling accurately* the word of truth" (II Tim. 2:15).

Finally, we pray that what we've written here has been guided by the love for truth, not motivated by a drive to "win an argument." God forbid that we should forsake reality for egotistic gain!

---

34. E.g., the second-chance salvation during the millennium; postponement of the victory of the cross; denying Jesus' contemporary kingship; God changes according to the way He deals with mankind (despite Heb. 13:8); reinstitution of Judaism, complete with temple and sacrifice; preferring future material glory to present spiritual blessing; God becomes a respecter of persons by race, etc. This applies especially to dispensational premillennialism.

BIBLIOGRAPHY

Adams, Jay. *Interpreting Revelation* (3 tape series). Fort Worth: Latimer House, n.d.

———. *The Time Is at Hand*. Philadelphia: Presbyterian and Reformed Publishing Co., 1966.

Ahlstrom, Sidney E. *A Religious History of the American People*. New Haven: Yale University Press, 1972.

Allis, Oswald T. *Prophecy and the Church*. Philadelphia: Presbyterian and Reformed Publishing Co., 1945.

———. *The Unity of Isaiah*. Philadelphia: Presbyterian and Reformed Publishing Co., 1977.

Augustine. *"The City of God," The Nicene and Post-Nicene Fathers*, ed. Philip Schaff. Grand Rapids: Wm. B. Eerdmans Publishing Co., 1977.

Baldwin, Marshall W. *The Mediaeval Church*. Ithaca: Cornell University Press, 1953.

Barclay, William. *The Revelation of John*, vols. 1 and 2. Philadelphia: Westminster Press, 1961.

Barker, William P. *Who's Who in Church History*. Grand Rapids: Baker Book House, 1969.

Berkhof, Louis. *The History of Christian Doctrines*. Grand Rapids: Baker Book House, 1937.

———. *Systematic Theology*. Grand Rapids: Wm. B. Eerdmans Publishing Co., 1953.

Bernstein, Leon. *Flavius Josephus—His Times and His Critics*. New York: Liveright Publishing Corp., 1938.

Bettenson, Henry, ed. *Documents of the Christian Church*. New York: Oxford University Press, 1976.

Biederwolf, William E. *The Second Coming Bible*. Grand Rapids: Baker Book House, 1977.

Boersma, T. *Is the Bible a Jigsaw Puzzle. . . .* St. Catherines, Ontario: Paideia Press, 1978.

Boettner, Loraine. *The Millennium*. Philadelphia: Presbyterian and Reformed Publishing Co., 1957.

Bright, John. *The Kingdom of God*. Nashville: Abingdon, 1953.

Calvin, John. *Calvin's New Testament Commentaries,* vols. 1-12. Grand Rapids: Wm. B. Eerdmans Publishing Co., 1978.

———. *Calvin's Commentaries* (O.T.), vols. 1-15. Grand Rapids: Baker Book House, 1979.

———. *Institutes of the Christian Religion,* vol. 1. Grand Rapids: Wm. B. Eerdmans Publishing Co., 1972.

Case, S. J. *The Millennial Hope*. Chicago: University of Chicago Press, 1918.

Chafer, L. S. *Dispensationalism*. Dallas: Dallas Seminary Press, 1936.

Clarke, Adam. *Clarke's Commentary*. Nashville: Abingdon, n.d.

Cox, William E. *Biblical Studies in Final Things*. Phillipsburg, N.J.: Presbyterian and Reformed Publishing Co., 1977.

Cunningham, William. *The Reformation and the Theology of the Reformation*. Carlisle, Pa.: The Banner of Truth Trust, 1979.

Darby, J. N. *Synopsis of the Books of the Bible,* vols. 1-5. Neptune, N.J.: Loizeaux Brothers, 1942.

Dodd, C. H. *The Parables of the Kingdom*. New York: Charles Scribner's Sons, 1961.

Durant, Will. *Age of Faith*. New York: Simon & Schuster, 1950.

———. *Caesar and Christ*. New York: Simon & Schuster, 1944.

———. *The Reformation*. New York: Simon & Schuster, 1957.

Ebeling, Gerhard. *Luther: An Introduction to His Thought*. Philadelphia: Fortress Press, 1970.

Edersheim, Alfred. *Old Testament Bible History*. Wilmington: Associated Publishers and Authors, Inc., n.d.

Fairbairn, Patrick. *Prophecy*. Grand Rapids: Baker Book House, 1976.

———. *The Prophetic Prospects of the Jews*. Grand Rapids: Wm. B. Eerdmans Publishing Co., 1930.

Fall of Jerusalem. London: T. Nelson & Sons, 1882.

Feinberg, Charles L. *Millennialism: The Two Major Views*. Chicago: Moody Press, 1980.

Forbush, W. B., ed. *Fox's Book of Martyrs*. Philadelphia: John C. Winston Co., 1926.

Ford, J. Massyngberde. *Revelation*. Garden City, N.Y.: Doubleday & Co., 1975.

Gaebelein, Arno C. *The Annotated Bible,* vols. 1-4. Neptune, N.J.: Loizeaux Brothers, 1970.

Grier, W. J. *The Momentous Event*. Carlisle, Pa.: The Banner of Truth Trust, 1945.

Halley, H. H. *Halley's Bible Handbook*. Grand Rapids: Zondervan Publishing Co., 1962. Copyright © 1965 by Halley's Bible Handbook, Inc.

Hendriksen, William. *More than Conquerors*. Grand Rapids: Baker Book House, 1939.

Hodge, Charles. *Systematic Theology,* vols. 1-3. Grand Rapids: Wm. B. Eerdmans Publishing Co., 1940.

Hoekema, Anthony A. *The Bible and the Future*. Grand Rapids: Wm. B. Eerdmans Publishing Co., 1979.

Huegel, F. J. *Reigning with Christ*. Minneapolis: Bethany Fellowship, Inc. (Dimension Books), 1963.

Hughes, Archibald. *A New Heaven and a New Earth*. Philadelphia: Presbyterian and Reformed Publishing Co., 1957.

Hughes, Philip E. *Interpreting Prophecy*. Grand Rapids: Wm. B. Eerdmans Publishing Co., 1976.

Josephus, Flavius. *"Wars of the Jews," Complete Works*. Grand Rapids: Kregel Publications, 1960.

Keller, Werner. *The Bible as History*. New York: William Morrow and Co., Publishers, 1956.

Kik, J. Marcellus. *An Eschatology of Victory*. Phillipsburg, N.J.: Presbyterian and Reformed Publishing Co., 1971.

Knox, John. *Christ the Lord*. New York: Harper and Row, 1945.

Ladd, George E. *Crucial Questions about the Kingdom of God*. Grand Rapids: Wm. B. Eerdmans Publishing Co., 1952.

———. *Jesus and the Kingdom*. Waco: Word Books, Publisher, 1964.

———. *The Last Things*. Grand Rapids: Wm. B. Eerdmans Publishing Co., 1978.

Latourette, Kenneth S. *Christianity through the Ages*. New York: Harper and Row, 1965.

Lehman, C. K. *The Fulfillment of Prophecy*. Scottdale, Pa.: Herald Press, 1971.

Lindsey, Hal. *The Late Great Planet Earth*. Grand Rapids: Zondervan Publishing House, 1970.

———. *Satan Is Alive and Well and Living on Planet Earth*. Grand Rapids: Zondervan Publishing House, 1972.

———. *There's a New World Coming*. Irvine, Calif.: Harvard House Publishers, 1973.

Lohse, Bernhard. *A Short History of Christian Doctrine*. Philadelphia: Fortress Press, 1966.

The Lost Books of the Bible. Collins World, 1977.

Luther, Martin. "Address to the Christian Nobility of the German Nation," *The Harvard Classics,* vol. 36. New York: P. F. Collier & Son Co., 1910.

Masselink, William. *Why Thousand Years?* Grand Rapids: Wm. B. Eerdmans Publishing Co., 1930.

McClain, Alva J. *Daniel's Prophecy of the Seventy Weeks*. Grand Rapids: Zondervan Publishing House, 1940.

McDowell, Edward A. *The Meaning and Message of the Book of Revelation*. Nashville: Broadman Press, 1951.

Mead, Frank S. *Handbook of Denominations*. Nashville: Abingdon, 1980.

Montgomery, John W. *History and Christianity*. Downers Grove, Ill.: InterVarsity Press, 1965.

Morgan, G. Campbell. Letter of 1943, *A New Heaven and a New Earth*. (Archibald Hughes) Philadelphia: Presbyterian and Reformed Publishing Co., 1957.

Mumford, Bob. *The King and You*. Old Tappan, N.J.: Fleming H. Revell Co., 1974.

Murray, G. L. *Millennial Studies: A Search for Truth*. Grand Rapids: Wm. B. Eerdmans Publishing Co., 1948.

New American Catholic Bible (notes). Washington, D.C.: The Confraternity of Christian Doctrine, Inc. 1970.

Orr, J. Edwin. *Evangelical Awakenings 1900—Worldwide*. Chicago: Moody Press, 1973.

Ortiz, J. C. *Call to Discipleship*. Plainfield, N.J.: Logos International, 1975.

———. *Cry of the Human Heart*. Carol Stream, Ill.: Creation House, 1977.

———. *Disciple*. Carol Stream, Ill.: Creation House, 1975.

Payne, H. L. "Amillennial Theology as a System." Unpublished doctoral dissertation. Dallas: Dallas Seminary Press, 1948.

Pentecost, J. Dwight. *Things to Come*. Grand Rapids: Zondervan Publishing House, 1958.

Pfeiffer, Charles F. *Old Testament History*. Grand Rapids: Baker Book House, 1973.

Quistorp, Heinrich. *Calvin's Doctrine of Last Things*. Atlanta: John Knox Press, 1955.

Radice, Betty, ed., Maxwell Staniforth, trans. *Early Christian Writings*. Harmondsworth, England: Penguin Books, Ltd., 1968.

Robertson, A. T. *A Harmony of the Gospels*. New York: Harper and Row, 1922.

Ryrie, C. C. *The Ryrie Study Bible* (notes). Chicago: Moody Press, 1978.

Sanday, William. *International Commentary on Romans*. New York: Scribners, 1896.

Sanford, John A. *The Kingdom Within*. New York: Paulist Press, 1970.

Sauer, Val J., Jr. *The Eschatology Handbook*. Atlanta: John Knox Press, 1981.

Scofield, C. I. *Rightly Dividing the Word of Truth*. Neptune, N.J.: Loizeaux Brothers, 1896.

———. *The Scofield Reference Bible* (notes). New York: Oxford University Press, 1909.

Scott, Walter. *Exposition of the Revelation of Jesus Christ*. London: Pickering and Inglis, 1948.

Shedd, W. G. T. *Dogmatic Theology*. New York: Scribners, 1891.

Sparks, Jack, ed. *The Apostolic Fathers*. Nashville: Thomas Nelson, Inc., Publishers, 1978.

Spitz, Lewis W. *The Renaissance and Reformation Movements*, vol. 2. St. Louis: Concordia Publishing House, 1971.

Summers, Ray. *The Life Beyond*. Nashville: Broadman Press, 1959.

———. *Worthy Is the Lamb*. Nashville: Broadman Press, 1951.

Tasker, R. V. G. *The Old Testament in the New Testament*. Grand Rapids: Wm. B. Eerdmans Publishing Co., 1946.

Tierney, Brian. *The Crisis of Church and State 1050–1300*. Englewood Cliffs, N.J.: Prentice-Hall, Inc., 1964.

Tillich, Paul. *A History of Christian Thought*. New York: Simon & Schuster, 1967.

Toynbee, Arnold. *A Study of History*. New York: Weathervane Books, 1972.

Vajta, Vilmos. *Luther on Worship*. Philadelphia: Fortress Press, 1958.

Vos, Geerhardus. *Biblical Theology*. Grand Rapids: Wm. B. Eerdmans Publishing Co., 1948.

———. *The Pauline Eschatology*. Grand Rapids: Wm. B. Eerdmans Publishing Co., 1972.

Walvoord, John. Article in *Bibliotheca Sacra*. Jan.–Mar., 1951.

———. *The Millennial Kingdom*. Findley, Ohio: Dunham Publishing Co., 1959.

Warfield, B. B. *Biblical Doctrines*. New York: Oxford University Press (copyright held by Presbyterian and Reformed Publishing Co., Phillipsburg, N.J.), 1929.

Webb, Myron T. *Startling Prophetic Events*. Montrose, Calif.: The Bible Fellowship Hour, n.d.

Whately, Richard. *The Kingdom of Christ*. New York: Wiley & Putnam, 1843.

White, Ellen. *The Great Controversy*. Washington, D.C.: Ellen G. White Publications (Mountain View, Calif.: Pacific Press), 1971.

Williams, Colin W. *John Wesley's Theology Today*. Nashville: Abingdon, 1960.

Williamson, G. A. *The World of Josephus*. London: Secker & Warburg, 1964.

Young, Edward J. *The Book of Isaiah*, vols 1-3. Grand Rapids: Wm. B. Eerdmans Publishing Co., 1965.

———. *The Prophecy of Daniel*. Grand Rapids: Wm. B. Eerdmans Publishing Co. 1949.

GLOSSARY

Amillennialism: the doctrine that the church community of the entire New Testament age is the spiritual kingdom known as the "millennium" of Revelation 20, where Jesus reigns as King over His people, Christian believers from every nation.

Apocalyptic literature: a form of Jewish writing (especially popular between the testaments) that is very mystical, full of symbolic language depicting catastrophe or magnificence and most often denoting the end of an age.

Apologetics: the branch of theology concerned with defending the Christian faith; sometimes used more broadly as argumentation in defense of any doctrine.

Chiliasm: derived from the Greek word for "thousand." It represents the teaching that the "millennium" of Revelation 20 is a future, physical, and utopian kingdom of 1000 years duration on earth; a synonym for premillennialism, but usually in reference to early church adherents.

Classical (or historical) premillennialism: the teaching that Christ's kingdom has already been inaugurated (begun) and will be consummated (perfected) at the second coming, introducing the utopian physical millennium on earth.

Comprehensivism: a branch of amillennialism that understands Bible prophecies concerning the kingdom (particularly Revelation) as being fulfilled in the church throughout the entire gospel age.

Dispensationalism: the branch of premillennialism that divides history into definite periods of time during which God deals with mankind in different ways according to His plan of redemption.

Eschatology: the study of the end times.

Exegesis: a critical method of Bible study (most often examining each Scripture verse by verse).

Great parenthesis: a dispensational doctrine encompassing the church age. It teaches that an indeterminate period of time occurs between Christ's resurrection and His second coming (after which He will establish the millennial kingdom). It is called a "parenthesis" because adherents claim there is no direct Old Testament prophecy describing this period of time: only the messianic kingdom is foretold, not the church.

Hermeneutic: any method of interpretation (e.g., literal, spiritual, symbolic).

Millennium: a word from the Latin meaning "thousand," used in reference to the "1000-year" kingdom in Revelation 20. Interpreted by premillennialists as a literal, future, utopian kingdom under Christ's rule on earth; by amillennialists as spiritual, contemporary kingdom of believers under Christ's lordship.

Olivet discourse: that portion of Scripture (Matt. 24, Mark 13, Luke 21) where Jesus answers His disciples' questions regarding the destruction of Jerusalem (A.D. 70). Others interpret this with reference to the end of the world.

Parousia: a transliteration of the Greek word for "appearing," generally applied to the second coming.

Postmillennialism: the doctrine that Jesus' second coming will follow the millennium, interpreted by adherents variously as regards its nature and duration.

Premillennialism: the teaching that Christ will establish a future, physical, utopian kingdom for 1000 years on earth after His second coming.

Preterism: a branch of amillennialism that understands all messianic prophecy concerning the kingdom as already fulfilled historically or being fulfilled spiritually in the church.

Rapture: the "catching up" of believers at Christ's appearing (the second coming) to meet Him in the air.

Realized eschatology: the teaching that the "last days" are contemporary to the church age, begun in apostolic times and continuing to the *parousia*.

Tribulation: according to premillennialists, that period of seven years (prior to the establishment of the millennium on earth) when unprecedented persecution and apostasy will take place under the aegis of the "Antichrist," or "Man of Sin." Otherwise interpreted as the Christian's spiritual battle against the forces of evil throughout the gospel age (by comprehensivist amillennialists) or as the events leading up to and culminating in the destruction of Jerusalem in A.D. 70 (by preterist amillennialists).

Two-age doctrine: the ancient Jewish teaching that saw Israel in two phases under God's eternal plan: their present (Old Testament) age of evil when Jews were under gentile subjection, and a future glorious age of national supremacy under the Messiah's reign.

INDEX OF NAMES

Adams, Jay, 39, 51, 60-61, 79, 83, 85, 90, 92, 99
Ahlstrom, Sidney, 33, 36
Allis, Oswald T., 29, 61, 71
Ambrose, St., 28
Antiochus Epiphanes, 77, 85
Aquinas, St. Thomas, 32, 33
Artaxerxes, 73
Athanasius, 27
Augustine, St., 4, 15, 28-29, 30, 33, 35, 93
Barclay, William, 4, 18, 19, 40, 52, 62, 97
Bellarmine, 35
Bengel, 38
Berkhof, Louis, 7, 24n, 27, 29, 30, 31, 90
Bernstein, Leon, 22
Boersma, T., 60, 65, 69, 72, 85, 90
Boettner, Loraine, 15, 38
Caius of Rome, 27
Calvin, John, 15, 23, 34, 35, 58, 61, 69
Case, S. J., 30
Chafer, Lewis, S., 89
Clarke, Adam, 58, 66, 69-70, 75
Clement of Alexandria, 26
Clement of Rome, 26
Comenius, 35
Constantine, 27
Coracio, 26
Cox, William E. (Ed), 9, 15, 16, 35, 39, 45, 55
Dante, 31
Darby, J. N., 15, 38, 97
Delitzsch, 38
Diocletian, 27
Dionysius, Exiguus, 74
Dionysius of Alexandria, 26
Dodd, C. H., 46, 96n
Dominic, 32
Domitian, 54n, 59n, 78, 85n
Douglas, James, 98
Durant, Will, 24, 25

Edward VI, 35-36
Eusebius, 26, 57, 79, 83
Feinberg, Charles, 8n
Forbush, W. B., 33n
Ford, J. Massyngberde, 18, 19, 28, 29, 30, 93
Francis of Assisi, 32
Grier, W. J., 27, 30n, 31n, 54, 56, 58, 88, 89, 90, 98
Halley, H. H., 95
Headlam, Arthur, 89
Hendriksen, William, 54, 90
Hermas, 25
Hippolytus, 25
Hodge, Charles, 9
Hoekema, Anthony A. 9, 64, 64-65, 68, 90, 96-97, 100
Hofmann, 38
Huegel, F. J., 93, 98
Hughes, Archibald, 62
Hughes, Philip E., 54
Huss, John, 33, 35
Ignatius, 15, 24, 27
Irenaeus, 23, 25
Jerome, 28
Joachim of Flora, 31
Josephus, 56, 57, 70, 77
Jurieu, 35
Justin (the) Martyr, 25
Kik, J. M., 38
Knox, John, 15, 35
Ladd, George Eldon, 4, 7, 39, 40, 88n, 89
Latourette, Kenneth Scott, 19, 28
Lehman, C. K., 89
Lindsey, Hal, 3, 39, 51n, 69, 97
Luther, Martin, 15, 32, 33, 34, 35
Masselink, William, 33
McDowell, Edward A., 50, 58, 80
Methodius, 25
Morgan, G. Campbell, 62
Mumford, Bob, 96n
Murray, G. L., 62

Nebuchadnezzar, 77, 84
Nepos, 25, 26
Nero, 40, 54n, 57, 58, 59, 78, 85, 97
Oetinger, 38
Origen, 15, 24, 26, 28
Orr, James, 41
Ortiz, Juan Carlos, 46-47, 102
Papias, 25, 26
Payne, H. L., 5
Pentecost, J. Dwight, 15, 97
Polycarp, 15, 26
Quistorp, Heinrich, 23
Rauschenbusch, 38
Ribera, 35
Rushdoony, R. J., 38
Sanday, William, 89
Sanford, J., 96n
Sauer, Val J., Jr., 88n
Scofield, C. I., 15, 38, 97
Scott, Walter, 8

Shedd, W. G. T., 31
Summers, Ray, 39
Tasker, R. V. G., 10n
Tatian, 27
Tertullian, 24, 25
Theophilus, 27
Titus, 20, 57, 75, 77
Tyconius, 27, 28
Vajta, Vilmos, 33
Vos, Geerhardus, 57-58, 90, 96
Walvoord, John, 35
Warfield, B. B., 92
Weigel, 35
Whately, Richard, 19-20
White, Ellen, 20, 56-57
Wright, H. F., 62
Wycliffe, John, 32, 33
Young, Edward J., 74, 75-76, 77
Zwingli, 35

INDEX OF SCRIPTURE

OLD TESTAMENT

Genesis
18:18—10, 16
49:1—72

Exodus
12—47

Leviticus
25:8—73

Numbers
12—7
24:14—72

Deuteronomy
2:34—34
18:18-19—62
29:4—18
30:8-10—90

Judges
5:19ff.—84

II Samuel
7:12—10
8:2—78

I Kings
8:13—77

II Kings
9:27—84

I Chronicles
28:7-9—62

II Chronicles
35:20-24—84
36:7—77

Ezra
7:11—73

Psalms
—102
2:9—34
16:8-11—10
51:16-17—74n
89:30-32—62
90:4—18
95:10—18
110:1-2—60
110:1-3—51
110:2—51

Isaiah
—17, 66, 102
1:11-13—22n
11:4—34
11:4-9—61
11:10—14n, 53
13:10—66
14:13—77
14:14—77
29:18—65
30—14n
35:5—65
40—61
49:6—17
53—16
54:13—61
60:1—28
61:1—65
65:17—61

Jeremiah
—17, 76
6:20—22n
23:20—72

25:11-12—73
29—17
31—14n
31:31-34—17
31:34—61

Ezekiel
—9, 17, 66, 85
11:19-20—17
18—16
20:38—90
32:7—66
33:29—76
38—61
38–39—85
38:16—72

Daniel
—6, 9, 17, 78, 102
2—16
2, 7, 10ff.—76, 79
2:35—100
2:41—84
2:44—63, 79, 97, 100
5:23—77
7:7—85
7:13—87
7:13-14—4, 69
7:19ff.—59
9—73, 76
9:24—73, 74, 75
9:26—74, 75
9:27—74, 75, 76
11:31—76
12:4, 9—79
12:11—76

Hosea
1:10—10

2:23—10
12—7

Joel
2—66
2:18—61
2:28-32—10, 70-71
2:30-31—7
3—16

Amos
9:11-12—10

Micah
1—16
4—14n
4:1—72
4:2—14n

Habakkuk
3—16

Zechariah
—102
2:11—14n

6:12, 13—51
9:9—10
14—16, 61

Malachi
1:10—22n
1:11—53
4:2—61

[APOCRYPHA]

I Maccabees
1:20-24—77

NEW TESTAMENT

Matthew
3:2—19
8:10-12—89
8:12—53
10:23—65
11—65
11:25—87
13:24-30—94
13:24-43—88
13:34-43—94
13:41, 43—94n
13:45-46—96
16:3—64
16:27—94
18:1-6—96
21—10
21:19—64
21:43—18, 19, 53
22:30—94
24—20, 54, 56, 57, 61, 65, 67, 68, 77, 112
24:3—65
24:7—70
24:15—76
24:16-20—57
24:21—55, 56
24:29—66
24:29-31—66, 70
24:30—68, 69, 87
24:34—70
24:37-39—86

25:31ff.—88
25:32—94
26:26-29—48
26:50—87
28:18—5, 96
28:18-20—93

Mark
1:15—19
9:12-13—7
10:30—73
13—56, 65, 67, 77, 112
13:14—76
13:26—87

Luke
2:11—87
2:35—87
3:23—74
7—65
7:20-22—96
8:4-15—96
10:9—19
10:18—53
11:14, 20—96
11:20—19
13:1—87
13:6-9—64
13:35—19
14:15-24—96
17—67

17:20—8
17:20-21—63
17:21—19, 47, 96
17:24, 26, 30—86
20:34-36—73
21—56, 65, 67, 77, 112
21:20, 21—20
21:20-24—83
21:24—78
21:27—87
21:29—64
21:31—8
22:16ff.—47
22:29—48
22:69—99, 103
24:39—47

John
—72
1:12—93
4:48—64
5:24-29—93
5:28-29—88, 93
6:39, 40, 44, 54—72
6:54—7
7:37—72
11:24—72, 94
12:31—53
12:32—4
12:48—72
14:12—93

16:7—98
16:12—7
18:36—19, 47, 96

Acts
1—21, 65
1:5—21
1:6—21
1:8—21
1:9—69
2—9, 10, 66, 72
2:16—71
2:19-20—7
2:22-36—21
2:23—18
2:30-31—10, 100
2:36—87
7:38—49
14:5—79n
14:16—54
15:13-18—10
17:1-9—79n
21:27ff.—79n
24:15—94

Romans
1:1-2, 9—14n
1:17—33
1:17, 18—87
2:16—95
2:28, 29—21, 62
5:17—98
8:22—71
9:6—21, 62
9:24-26—10
11—90
11:11—18
11:13—21
11:24—90
11:25—13n, 89
11:26—90
12:1—74n
14:10—94
14:17—47

I Corinthians
1:7—86
3:16—99
10:11—73

13:12—62
15:24—50, 94n
15:24-25—5
15:25—51, 60
15:50—47

II Corinthians
3:6—8
5:21—78

Galatians
2:20—93
3:8—10, 16
4:21-31—21
4:26—51
4:28—21
5:17—59
6:16—89

Ephesians
1:9—13n
1:21—73
2:4-6—93
2:14—92
3:5—87
5:27—5
6:12—55, 57

Philippians
1:26—87
2:7—34
2:11—87
2:13—98
3:20—48

Colossians
1:13—21
2:2—13n
2:15—53

I Thessalonians
3:13—87
4:16-17—72n
5:3—87

II Thessalonians
—58
1:7—86
2:3-4—58
2:7—34

II Timothy
2:15—103
4:1—87
4:8—87

Titus
2:13—87

Hebrews
—22, 26
1:2—72, 98
2:5—73
2:14—53
5:12—103
7:17—97
7:27—74
8:1, 2—51
8:2—77
8:2, 5—49
8:5-6—97
8:8-12—17
9:11, 12—75
9:12—22
9:14—74
9:26—72, 74
10:4—97
10:12—97
12:22—51
12:28—48, 97
13:8—103n

James
4:4—59
4:7—98
5:3—72

I Peter
1:5—72n
1:7, 13—87
1:20—72
2:2—103
2:5—60, 99
2:9—48
5:8—53

II Peter
1:16—87
3:3—72
3:8—18

3:10—86
3:12—86
3:12-13—61

I John
—58
2:18—58, 72
2:22—58
4:4—54
5:4-5—51

II John
—58

Revelation
—6, 9, 18, 34, 51, 52, 54, 55, 57, 59, 77, 78, 79, 80, 81, 82, 83, 85, 92, 111
1—52
1–19—52
1:1—78n, 82
1:3—55
1:5—4, 22, 50, 99
1:5-6—5
1:6—22, 60
1:9—22, 55
1:19—78n, 80
2–3—78, 80
2, 7, 10ff.—79
2–19—79
4, 5, 7, 11, 19—83
4–5—83
4–19—55, 78
4–22—78
5:10—5
7—83
7:4-8—83
9—51
9:6—51
11—83
11:1—78
11:2—78
13—58
13:3—58, 85n
13:3, 14—85n
13:18—59n, 78
16—84, 86
17—84
17:5—85
17:8, 11—85n
20—3n, 4, 18-19, 50, 55, 61, 78, 80, 84, 85, 93, 94, 95, 111, 112
20:1—8
20:1-6—8, 40
20:2—59
20:2-3—52
20:3—60, 90
20:4—51, 93
20:4-6—19
20:5-6—92
20:7-8—55, 60
20:7-10—84
20:14—93
21, 22—61, 78
22:10—55, 79n

27366

DATE DUE

BT 891 .R8 1982

27366

The ruler of the kings of the earth.

HIEBERT LIBRARY
Fresno Pacific College - M. B. Seminary
Fresno, Calif. 93702